Ho[illegible]me the Oxford Open Learning Way

Andrew Johnson

Oxford Open Learning

Additional material by Dr Nicholas Smith

Illustrations by David Benham
43 Ulfgar Road
Wolvercote
Oxford OX2 8BA
tel/fax 01865 556714

First published in 1999 by
OOL
4 King's Meadow
Oxford OX2 0DP
England

A catalogue record for this book is available from
the British Library.

ISBN 0-9536079-0-9

Typeset in 11/14 Bookman.
Printed in Great Britain by Welton Print Ltd, Royal Leamington Spa.

CONTENTS

INTRODUCTION

Welcome to the Oxford Open Learning way

Congratulations! You've decided to embark on a course of home study. Whether you're doing this to upgrade your qualifications and skills, to improve your job prospects or to make yourself a better-informed individual, this book offers you help and advice about when, where and how to study.

Deciding that you want to study is the easy part, but seeing that decision through by completing your course and passing the exams is not so easy. How can you make sure you keep at it and pass your exams? Studying at home will test your determination as well as your learning power. *How to Study at Home the Oxford Open Learning Way* shows you how you can overcome the difficulties that lie in your path and be a winner!

What is the Oxford Open Learning home study way?

The key to the Oxford Open Learning way is the idea of learning by doing. Too many textbooks allow students to sit passively trying to absorb facts, without really *doing* anything. This is not the best way to learn. For a student to learn effectively, he or she needs to be actively engaged in the learning process. That's why Oxford Open Learning's course packs, as well as this Study Guide, contain plenty of activities for you to do.

About this book

This study guide is aimed at everyone who is studying at home. It is intended in particular for students who are using Oxford Open Learning's GCSE and 'A' level study packs. Some sections of Chapter 4 are aimed specifically at these students, but most of the advice and activities will also be of use if you are studying in a different situation.

Oxford Open Learning has supported many thousands of home learners over the years and in these pages you'll learn some of the secrets we've discovered along the way.

How to Study at Home the Oxford Open Learning Way is packed full of useful advice, and there are regular practical activities which will enable you to develop all the skills you need to make a success of your studies.

This book begins by showing you how to set up a suitable study environment. It then helps you to design and implement your Study Plan. Later chapters offer advice about developing your study skills, planning your revision and dealing with stressful situations. The final chapter gives you essential information about how to prepare for your exams.

How to use this book

How you use this book is up to you. The less sure you are about your study skills, the more you should consider working through it systematically, chapter by chapter, doing as many of the activities as you find useful.

Otherwise, you can think of it as a handy guide, to be dipped into when you need specific advice or when you are struggling for inspiration. Keep it nearby and refer to it often!

The Oxford Open Learning Study Skills Certificate

If you work through a significant number of the activities in this book and master the skills of studying at home, you become eligible for the Oxford Open Learning Study Skills Certificate.

Simply send a folder of your work to:

The Course Director
Oxford Open Learning
4 King's Meadow
Oxford OX2 0BD

The folder must contain answers to at least 20 of the activities in this book, and at least 2000 words in total. There is no upper limit to length. Make sure that the chapter and activity numbers are clearly indicated on each sheet.

Your folder will be approved and a certificate will be issued to you. This may be of help to you in gaining entry to certain future programmes of study.

Oxford Open Learning regrets that the folder of work must be retained by Oxford Open Learning and cannot be returned to you. So please make a copy of all your answers before you send in your work.

Any comments you have about this study guide may also be posted to the above address, or you can send your opinions by e-mail to studyguide@ool.co.uk.

Good study skills are an asset for life and a necessity for the successful student. Whether or not you plan to apply for a Study Skills Certificate later on, congratulations on your determination to improve your study skills!

Acknowledgements

My thanks are due to David Benham, who drew the cartoons, Marie Oxenbould, our print consultant, Gary Lewis of Welton Print, and Mark Seymour for his design work. I would also like to thank all my colleagues at Oxford Open Learning who offered advice, including Dr Nicholas Smith, Principal, Amanda Blunden, Administrative Director, Jonathan Smith, Financial Director, Greg Smith, Head of Operations, Linda Kerr, College Programmes Manager and Moya Hughes, Tuition Services Manager.

If you'd like to know more about the range of subjects available from Oxford Open Learning, simply call 0870 789 0800 and ask for a prospectus.

Good luck, and enjoy your studies!

Andrew Johnson
June 1999

1 YOU AND YOUR ENVIRONMENT

A YOUR SELF-IMAGE

How do you feel about yourself?

How effectively do you study? The answer will depend on many factors. One of the most important is how you feel about what you are doing. If you feel sick, or if you're tired, bored, or hungry, it's obvious that you won't be able to study properly. Yet it's amazing how many people ignore their bodies' basic needs when they set out on a course of study!

You can look after your health by making sure that you get enough exercise and enough sleep, and by eating regular, nutritious meals. In the same way, you can look after your state of mind, which includes your *self-image*, nearly as easily. We all experience times of crisis in our lives, and we all know what it's like to feel worried or miserable. But if you constantly feel insecure your mind will be distracted and your ability to study will be affected.

Think positive!

Feeding yourself good food helps to keep your body in good shape. In the same way, feeding yourself positive thoughts and adapting your study environment will improve your self-confidence. Negative thoughts, on the other hand, will undermine your self-confidence and damage your self-image.

Almost everybody has more potential than they realise. Plenty of people prevent themselves from learning just because they don't believe in their own abilities. Believing in yourself can be a source of enormous strength. It's a question of attitude. A calm, quiet approach will lead to confidence and success.

The danger of over-confidence

Some people suffer from the opposite problem: over-confidence. This is often just an excuse for doing nothing. You fool yourself that your course is easy and requires little effort. So you do nothing until a month before the exam. Then you suddenly turn into the anxious, nervous, frightened kind of student. But now you have reason to be anxious, because you haven't done any work!

In practice, problems of over-confidence and over-anxiety can be avoided. There are two solutions which work together, and they are *motivation* and *organisation*. This chapter will explore both.

ACTIVITY 1

Do as few or as many of the activities in this book as you like. Try to do some of them, so as to practise your skills. Write down your answers and keep them in a file for future reference.

1. Look at the three cartoons of open learners studying on pages 2, 3 and 4.
2. Which one of these learners is the most organised?
3. What kinds of errors are the others making in organising their time and their learning environment?

ACTIVITY 2

1. What kind of person are you? Think of three or four adjectives that describe yourself.
2. How do you feel about your studies?

3. What are your study problems?
4. What can you do to solve or minimise each of these problems?
5. Whose advice can you ask to help you solve your study problems?
6. How motivated are you in your studies?
7. What can you do to focus or improve your motivation?
8. How organised are you?
9. What can you do to become more organised?

B TURNING PROBLEMS INTO OPPORTUNITIES

Where do I begin?

Studying is a practical business, the business of acquiring knowledge and skills. There's nothing very mysterious about it, as long as your approach is systematic. And if you are motivated and organised, there's no reason why you shouldn't enjoy your studies, too.

Of course, some parts of your syllabus will be more interesting than others. But in general, learning about the world and how it works should be exciting. Children are naturally inquisitive: their minds soak up everything around them. Think of how effortlessly they learn language!

As we get older most of us tend to experiment less, to become less open to new ideas. But it's possible, with a little effort, to keep that spark of curiosity alive.

Getting started

When I first sat down to start writing this book, I achieved absolutely nothing during the first three days. The task seemed too big. Right now, you may well be embarking on a course of study. Perhaps you're also feeling a bit daunted by the apparently huge task ahead.

Beginning is always difficult, so I made up an activity to get my mind focused on the work ahead. First, I'll describe the activity. Then I'll give you my own response to it, as an example. After you've read through the activity and my response, try it yourself. It only takes five or ten minutes. (You may not want to go into as much detail as I have done – this was just to make the activity as clear as possible.) How similar or different are your answers and mine?

ACTIVITY 3

1. Imagine you are preparing to start a session of study.
2. How do you feel? (Refer back to Activity 1 if you want to.)
3. Write down five or six adjectives to describe your state of mind at the moment. (Write longer notes if you want to.)
4. Now look at the list.
5. Which words or phrases are positive? (Write '**P**' next to these.)
6. Which words are negative? (Write '**N**' next to these.)
7. Look at any positive words. No problems here! You want more of these!
8. Look at any negative words. Think about the reasons why you feel this way.
9. Can you replace any negative words with positive ones, and so improve your self-image?

MY ANSWERS TO ACTIVITY 3

I feel:

1. excited about the project (P);
2. worried that I won't get all my ideas down on paper (N);
3. tired after a late night watching TV (N);
4. annoyed that I've already been interrupted twice this morning (N);
5. more-or-less confident that I have the ability to do the job well (P).

That gives me three negatives and two positives. What can I do about the negatives?

2. Relax! Keep a notebook nearby so you can record new ideas. It doesn't matter what order the ideas come in. Think about Answer No. 5 and reassure yourself that you will be able to arrange your thoughts more logically later on.
3. Go to bed earlier, especially if you have any thinking to do the next day!
4. Ask the people you share space with not to disturb you while you are busy. Specify the hours when you won't be available. At the same time make sure that you set aside some time each day, or every few days, when you will interact with them (have a coffee, watch TV together, or just talk).

One day at a time

And finally, don't panic! This is only the beginning, and there's a long way to go. Divide the big task into small sections and the project will start to look more manageable. One day at a time!

Keep a record of your studies

Another way of boosting your self-confidence is to keep a record of what you have achieved (see the example on page 9). If you feel unmotivated, start by checking through your list of accomplishments. You can't cover the whole syllabus in one day, or one month. You have to work through the topics gradually and methodically. By keeping a note of what you've done, you will realise that as days go by you are learning more and more and increasing your chances of success.

Reward yourself

If you have a record of what you've achieved, you can measure your progress and then set more realistic goals in the future. And when planning ahead, why not reward yourself for a particular task completed? For example:

Phillipa said to herself: 'I'm going to read Chapter 7 of my 'A' level Psychology textbook. Then I'm going to eat a bar of chocolate.'

Ibrahim decided: 'I'm going to work on French verbs for an hour a day every day this week. On Saturday night I'm going to forget all about French and go clubbing.'

November
WEEK 46 1999

	Planned	Achieved
15 MONDAY	1 hour - 'A' Level Biology	½ Hour 'A' Level Biology
16 TUESDAY	1 Hour - 'A' Level Biology 1 Hour - GCSE Mathematics	1 Hour - 'A' Level Biology ½ Hour - GCSE Mathematics
17 WEDNESDAY (321-44)	2 Hours - GCSE Mathematics	1½ Hours - GCSE Mathematics

November
1999 WEEK 46

	Planned	Achieved
THURSDAY 18	1 Hour - 'A' Level Biology	1½ Hour 'A' Level Biology
FRIDAY 19	½ Hour GCSE Mathematics	½ Hour GCSE Mathematics
SATURDAY 20	½ Hour GCSE Mathematics	½ Hour GCSE Mathematics
SUNDAY 21	DAY OFF Notes: I planned to do this studying and got behind but caught up a bit towards the end of the week	DAY OFF Total Hours studied 6½ Not Bad!!

999 2000

Alan thought: 'I'll work through this GCSE Maths paper until eight o'clock. Then I'll meet my mates in the pub for a game of pool.'

Sarah told her husband: 'As soon as I've finished reading through my Business Studies syllabus, marking the tricky parts, I'll make us both a toasted sandwich and then watch *Brookside* with you.

Shefali decided that she wouldn't telephone her brother, Krish, for a chat, until she had finished Lesson 8 of her 'A' level Biology study pack, on nutrition, and had also answered the self-test questions at the end.

How to SWOT!

We've talked about improving your self-image. Now let's look at your studies from a wider perspective. Business managers often do what they call a SWOT analysis, either to understand the stage their present business has reached, or to help them decide on a new venture. But you can do a SWOT analysis to clarify almost any situation. It's a great way of turning difficulties into opportunities. I even know someone who did a SWOT analysis before asking his girlfriend to marry him!

SWOT stands for:

- Strengths
- Weaknesses
- Opportunities
- Threats

Chapter 2 of this book shows how to organise your study time, and also deals with goals and motivation. Now, however, let's do a SWOT analysis of your present study situation in order to help you examine your self-image. This exercise uses a similar approach to Activity 3 above, but also takes other factors into consideration.

ACTIVITY 4

1. Divide a blank sheet of A4 paper into four equal sections, using a ruler.
2. Label each quarter with one of these headings: Strengths, Weaknesses, Opportunities and Threats.
3. Think about the four words in turn, and write brief notes under each heading about yourself and how you relate to your studies.

Again, I've used my own situation in writing this book as an example:

Strengths

- I already have a coherent plan.
- I know most of what I want to say.
- I have experience of this kind of work.

Weaknesses

- I write too much.
- There's a danger that some of what I write is not relevant.
- Sometimes I don't feel motivated.
- Writing is hard work: I'd rather stop and go for a walk.

Opportunities

- I have plenty of time.
- I'm lucky to have a pleasant room in which to work.
- I can write a book that will help students and also help my career.
- Writing about study techniques should help my own powers of study.

Threats

- I find it difficult to concentrate. I get distracted easily.
- I watch too much TV.
- I worry about my personal life and that gets in the way of work.

Look at what I have written under the headings 'Weaknesses' and 'Threats'. What could I do to turn these negative aspects of my situation into positive ones?

Now make your own list, like mine, but about *your* present study situation. When you have finished, think about how to turn negatives into positives. If there is anybody nearby who is willing to discuss your list with you, ask them to help.

C YOUR STUDY ENVIRONMENT

The need for privacy

We all lead busier, noisier, more interrupted lives than in the past. Radio, TV, videos and computers may be wonderful inventions, but they can invade our privacy just as much as other people. And although worthwhile study can take place in groups (discussions, debates), solitude and privacy are essential ingredients of any successful study programme. Nowadays it's more difficult than ever for most of us to find a quiet place to study, or even just to read a book in peace. This section is all about finding or making an environment that suits you, one that will help you to maximise your potential for efficient and enjoyable study.

ACTIVITY 5

1. Write a brief description (if you like drawing you could draw a picture as well or instead) of the place you normally use for studying.
2. Now write a brief description (or draw a picture) of your imaginary perfect place for study.
3. Compare the two descriptions or pictures. What are the differences? Are there luxuries in the imaginary description or picture that you don't really need? If so, leave out these details.
4. Now think of practical ways of improving your existing study place to make it more like your ideal one.

ACTIVITY 6

Here's another, related activity.

1. Make a list of all the equipment you need to be able to study effectively at home. (You don't need to include equipment that is provided for you, such as test tubes in a chemistry laboratory, or a dead rat for dissection in Biology.)
2. When you've finished, compare your list to my list, which appears at the very end of this chapter.
3. Don't look at my list until you've completed your own!

My list assumes that you are studying mainly in your own home, although you may be spending most of your study time in a library or an office. Remember that some equipment (such as a pair of compasses) is only needed for certain subjects. Can you think of any items you need for your subject that I have omitted from my list?

Sometimes we have no choice but to study in an environment that is far from perfect. Under such circumstances we have to do our best to turn problems into opportunities. For example, the musician and composer, Béla Bartók, was living in central Europe during the First World War. The war disrupted his life so that it was difficult for him to compose his music. One particular problem was the shortage of candles. Bartók had other work to do during the day, so he could only compose at night. So he sat at one end of the kitchen table writing music, while his son sat at the other end doing his homework. Two candles stood between father and son, in the middle of the table, giving them both just enough light to work by.

Besides some basic essentials for study, which we can probably all agree on, we have to remember that different people have very different habits and preferences. Your ideal study environment might be my worst nightmare. Some people need total silence to study, while others appear to be able to work and think to the accompaniment of earth-shatteringly noisy rock music.

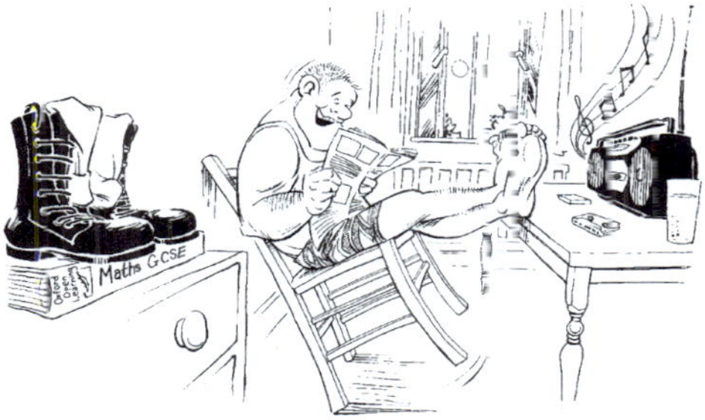

Some teachers believe that classical music not only soothes the soul and focuses the attention, but actually stimulates mental activity. I know several people who regularly use Mozart's music for this purpose in workshops and seminars, and they say that it works.

DESPERATE MEASURES!

Some learners claim that they can study and watch TV at the same time. In my opinion, if a TV is on in a room, it's virtually impossible to concentrate on anything else. So my advice is, either work in a room where there is no TV, or switch it off! Having a telephone in your room can also be disruptive. If someone phones you when you're busy, tell them so, and unless it's urgent, ask them to phone back later.

Arrange your space

You need to be organised in two basic ways: *time* and *space*. (Chapter 2, Section B deals with how to organise your time.)

Once you've got your room stocked with the necessary equipment, you need to work out how to make best use of the space available. That involves classifying and storing all your information so that you can find it and reach it easily when you need it.

File your notes

Most people buy files or folders and label each one according to the subjects they are studying. You can use colour-coded marker pens or sticky labels to distinguish one subject from another. To save money, I have stored my notes for this book in used A4 manila envelopes, one for each chapter.

If the syllabus of your subject falls into clearly defined sections (this will usually be the case) you could label one folder or envelope for each section. In 'A' level Law, for example, you could have one folder for each of these main topics:

- The idea of law and its social aspects
- Parliamentary and judicial law-making
- Dispute solving and liability
- Specific liability and sanctions
- The law of contract

Make an index

You could arrange files for a particular subject either in alphabetical order or in the order in which they appear on the syllabus. It doesn't really matter, as long as you have a system that makes sense to you. Make a list (or index) of all your files, and keep the index in a place where you can always find it. Your index should list files in the same order in which they are stored.

Store your study packs and files nearby

Having created files to suit the subjects and topics you are studying, you should keep them in a filing cabinet, on a shelf, or in a box. All your study materials should be stored close at hand and within easy reach of your desk.

Brighten up your place of study

Make your working environment as attractive and comfortable as possible. Arrange your desk so that you can see out of a window, or decorate the wall in front of you with posters. Place photos of your friends and family nearby.

You can brighten up your environment and provide yourself with study aids at the same time. You could write your main reason for studying on a brightly coloured notice and place it where you will see it every day (see Section A of Chapter 2 for more about motivation). You could place your timetable or Study Plan (see Chapter 2, Section B), with details entered in different colours, on the wall in front of you. Or you could design an activity chart, which presents the same information in a pictorial or diagrammatic form. You could even make a set of coloured charts that summarise topics from your course, and change these around from time to time. (See Chapter 6, Section A for advice on the importance of planning your revision strategy and starting your revision early on in your studies. Also see Chapter 3, Section C for help using visual aids to improve your memory.)

Guard against interruptions

Your efforts to create a suitable study space may be ruined if you are continually interrupted. People who have studied recently or are studying at present should be sympathetic.

But it may be that you share your living space with people who don't know or care how much self-discipline and determination studying requires. You will have to explain to them that you need privacy and peace to be able to complete your course.

As far as possible, specify times when everyone knows you will be busy studying. Set aside different times when you will be available to interact with others. The important thing is to establish mutual respect and understanding, so that you are able to fulfil your domestic and social obligations at certain times of the day, leaving you free to study at other times.

If you can't study at home

Studying at home may for some reason be difficult or impossible. If you don't have the basic equipment necessary, if there is no quiet room where you can work, or if there are domestic difficulties at home, you may be better off studying in your local library. If you are employed, and you have access to an office, you may be allowed to study there during your free time, but ask permission first. If you approach your employer you may find that he or she is more sympathetic than you expected. Don't do your studying during working hours, however, or you may get fired!

D PUTTING IT ALL TOGETHER

Adopting an integrated approach

You need to adopt an *integrated* approach to your studies – one that takes account of all aspects of your situation. It means keeping the big picture in mind, and not taking details out of context. In this chapter we have begun to look at some elements of your whole situation – how you feel about yourself and where you do most of your studying. In later chapters we will talk about the integrated approach again, but for now the point I want to make is that you need to be realistic about *how much* studying you can do.

Your study time has to fit into the routine of your daily life. This is a pattern which includes all your responsibilities and obligations. As well as studying, it's essential to leave enough time to relax, to be with your friends, to eat and sleep well, and to have a good time.

Look after yourself

Your body is a very delicate instrument, and it deserves to be treated well and properly looked after. If you don't put any engine oil in your car, you shouldn't be surprised if it breaks down. Your body also needs regular upkeep and attention.

So the integrated approach really just means, look after yourself, and keep things in perspective! Don't try to study all night. You'll waste two days recovering! When you're studying hard, you're probably using more energy than at other times. That means you need to take extra care over sleep, recreation and nutrition.

Make sure you get plenty of exercise. If you play sport, build your sporting interests into your timetable. If you don't like sport, practise some other form of exercise, such as yoga, or aerobics, or go for regular walks. Different individuals need different amounts of sleep, and only *you* know how much sleep you need. And take extra care to eat healthy, nutritious food. Your brain needs to be kept well supplied!

When you're studying, you will probably need to change your lifestyle to find time for the additional work. Most people are busier than they think. If you need to make changes, do so gradually. Find 45 minutes of study time per day to begin with, and only increase the amount when you have got used to studying regularly. (See Chapter 2, Section B for further details.) Take your studies seriously, but don't allow them total domination over your life!

MY LIST OF STUDY EQUIPMENT (See ACTIVITY 6)

⮝ only needed for certain subjects
❄ needed by some people more than others

About the room

- light
- fresh air when it's warm (ventilation)
- heating when it's cold
- privacy
- dry walls, floor, ceiling and work-surfaces (dampness is the enemy of books and papers)
- door that you can shut if necessary (doesn't apply if you're working in a library)
- ❄ quiet (some people can study with music playing)
- ❄ something pleasant to look at, but not distracting (view from a window, or a poster or picture you like)

Furniture

- table or desk large enough to spread papers on (at least 3 feet wide and 2 feet deep) and of a height to suit you
- comfortable upright or office chair
- bookshelf
- ❄ filing cabinet
- ❄ armchair or easy chair, if possible, for when you are reading but do not need to sit at a desk
- desk lamp or other suitable light (don't work in your own shadow)

Stationery

- notebooks, blank paper, lined paper, scrap paper
- pens and pencils
- ruler, eraser, pencil sharpener
- stapler
- paper clips
- folders, files, large envelopes
- correction fluid
- ⮝ graph paper, squared paper
- ❄ paper stickers
- ❄ coloured markers, highlighters

Books and documents

- your study pack
- dictionary
- subject-specific reference books, e.g. atlas, glossary of literary terms
- syllabus
- past exam papers
- ⮝ thesaurus
- ⮝ additional textbooks

Mechanical and electrical equipment

- watch or clock
- ⮝ computer and floppy disks
- ⮝ mathematical instruments
- ⮝ calculator
- ⮝ cassette player

2 TOWARDS A STUDY PLAN

A GOALS AND MOTIVATION

Why study?

In Chapter 1 we discussed your self-image and your study environment. We also looked at the need for an integrated approach. We found that effective learning depends on managing your time well and integrating regular study periods into your weekly routine.

This chapter begins by exploring *motivation*. If you can keep focused on *why* you want the qualification you seek, and keep that goal always in mind, you will find that your studying becomes more purposeful and rewarding.

People have different habits and preferences when it comes to where, when and how to study. Our reasons for studying also vary enormously. What are you studying, and why? Here are some answers.

Phillipa Kelly says: 'I got pregnant at 16 and left school with only two GCSE passes. I had another baby two years later. Then the children's father went off with another woman. I haven't seen him since. Life for single mothers can be really hard.

Ever since I left school I've been wanting to go back to studying. When I told my sister about this, she offered to look after my children for two afternoons a week to give me some time to myself. That was two years ago. First I did my GCSE Maths and English Literature with Oxford Open Learning. Now I'm studying 'A' level Psychology because my ambition is to do a degree in Psychology with the Open University.'

Ibrahim Mahmoud says: 'I work for a computer software company in Huddersfield. For a long time now I've been looking to improve my salary. I've applied for several other jobs but haven't had any luck. Then a couple of months ago my boss said that our company was planning to open an office in Senegal. I was told I had a chance of a management post there, on a much higher salary, if I could speak a bit of French. I got six GCSEs at school but I failed French. So I've enrolled with Oxford Open Learning to retake French in the hope of furthering my career and getting the chance to see Africa!'

Sarah Moss says: 'I've been working as a sales assistant in a hardware store for ten years. I never had much time for school work because I always had to help my mum look after my younger brothers and my little sister. Then last month my boss said she would consider offering me the job of assistant manager if I got some business qualifications. So I've just enrolled with Oxford Open Learning to do GCSE Accounting and Business Studies.'

Alan Carter says: 'When I was at school I never took much notice of what the teachers said. I thought school was a waste of time. But after three years of unemployment I got fed up with sitting around. My girlfriend even left me because I couldn't afford to take her out. So I decided to join the army and make something of my life. And now I've found a career, I want to get myself promoted. I don't want to be a private all my life. But that won't happen unless I get some qualifications. So I've made a start by enrolling with Oxford Open Learning. I'm doing GCSE Maths and English, because these are the key subjects. When I've passed these subjects, I'm going to do Chemistry and Physics next.'

Shefali Bhagat says: 'I'm working in my father's shoe shop in Birmingham. I got three GCSE passes at school but that was five years ago and I've forgotten it all now. Then one of my friends told me about Oxford Open Learning – she's doing her 'A' levels with them. So I looked at the Biology study pack and I decided to enrol too. Biology's a fascinating subject. The work is quite difficult, and there are lots of unfamiliar concepts, but 'A' level is much more challenging than GCSE. I have no idea what I want to do eventually, but at least I've found a subject that really interests me.'

ACTIVITY 1

Think about the different reasons that Phillipa, Ibrahim, Sarah, Alan and Shefali have for studying. Do you have anything in common with any of them?

Here are some questions about *your* motivation. Write answers to them on a sheet of paper. (As I suggested in Chapter 1, it would be useful for you to open a file on *How to Study: Activities* and keep your answers to activity questions safely for future reference.)

1. What are you studying?
2. Why are you studying these subjects?
3. What are your short-term goals?
4. What are your long-term goals?
5. How much effort are you prepared to put into your work to ensure that you succeed?
6. Share your ideas with anyone who is willing to discuss them with you.
7. How realistic are your goals?
8. Can you do anything to make them more attainable?

If you can't come up with a good reason for studying, you probably aren't really committed to the task. If you have a strong reason for doing something, you are more likely to succeed. If you have a reason to study, keep focused on that reason as much as possible. One way of doing this is to design an attractive notice or poster that summarises your overall goal. You can display this in a place where you will see it every day.

Focus on motivation

There are many good reasons for studying, but most of them fall in one of these three categories:

- academic requirements (for example, to enter university)
- to improve your job or career prospects
- personal fulfillment and pleasure

You're probably studying for one or two of these reasons. In some ways, the first reason provides the easiest source of motivation. You might remind yourself, for example, that if you get anything less than a C grade at 'A' level Maths you'll miss the chance of going to the university of your dreams.

If you're studying in order to improve your job prospects, the situation is a bit different. In most cases, you won't know for sure that studying now will help you to get the job you want in two years' time, or that you will eventually earn more money. When your spirits are low, such a goal can seem rather vague. But in the long term, improving your qualifications really will make a difference to your employment prospects and earning power.

Research has shown that, in terms of your expected earnings, each 'A' level you achieve is worth £2000 a year for the rest of your life, while each GCSE is worth about £700 a year. Think of what you could do with that extra money! Keep in mind this extra earning power if ever your motivation begins to falter.

If your are studying entirely for personal fulfillment, you will probably need to rely on the fact that you find study pleasurable and your subject interesting. Work out what you enjoy most about the subject and draw on that when you need support.

When the going gets tough

Sometimes the final goal looks very far away. Learning all the information you need, acquiring all the skills, completing all the coursework on time, and eventually passing those dreaded exams – it all seems so much! When things are going well, all you have to do is stick to your Study Plan (see Section B of this chapter). But there may be times when you feel as if you're not making any progress, when it all seems too difficult, or there doesn't seem to be enough time.

When this happens, you have to take a deep breath, relax, and remember *why* you are studying. You may find it helpful to review or even re-do Activity 1 of this chapter from time to time. And don't forget that your tutor and your student adviser are always there for you. Telephone them whenever you need to (see Chapter 4, Sections A and B).

Sitting isn't studying

Some people spend all their time preparing to study, but they never get started. An hour later, the study period finishes, and they think they've achieved something, but they haven't.

This is a question of conditioning. If you are in the habit of sitting at your desk and doing very little, you need to 're-program' yourself to a different kind of behaviour. Set yourself brief (10 – 20 minute) tasks at first, and keep a note of what you achieve. Then build up your concentration time gradually. If this doesn't work, try studying in a different place, such as a library.

A little at a time

If your long-term goal seems overwhelming, break it up into a series of short-term goals. If you wanted to be a champion athlete, you would have to practise daily. Similarly, you have to make an ongoing commitment to your studies. You can't do it all today, or tomorrow, or (the worst idea of all) the day before the exam. Practice makes perfect: do a little at a time.

Regularity is essential. Having designed your Study Plan, do your utmost to keep to it. You need some time off each week, but that should be built into your timetable in the first place (see Section C below).

Some students begin their courses with great enthusiasm, but after a few months they lose their way, neglecting their Study Plan and falling behind. If you miss just *one* study session, for whatever reason, remind yourself of your reasons for doing your course. Discuss them with friends or family. Phone your tutor for advice. Design and display a new poster that you will look at every day (also see Chapter 5, Section D).

Julia the violinist

Here's another story. I once had a girlfriend who was studying modern languages but who wanted to become a professional musician. I was studying English. I read my set books and did my assignments. I wanted to spend all my spare time with Julia. But she was doing a degree in languages *and* training to become a violinist. She played her violin for six hours a day. Often she didn't have time to talk to me at all. Sometimes I was allowed to sit in her room and read while she practised Bach.

Then one day I told her I was fed up with playing second fiddle to a lump of wood and she had to choose between me and her stupid violin. Of course, she chose the violin, and that was the end of that. Julia went on to fulfil her ambitions. She got her degree in languages and is now a professional musician in a touring string quartet.

I hope that this story puts doing an open learning course into perspective. You may be battling with your studies at the moment, and there are bound to be difficult moments ahead. We all go through bleak times. You need motivation and commitment, and you need to be organised, but you don't have to spend all day with your nose in your study pack. Take it day by day, a little at a time.

A learning contract

In effect, you have made a learning contract simply by committing yourself to a course of study. Your learning contract is your personal Study Plan. It includes details of the subject you have chosen to study, the syllabus you are working towards and the examination date you are aiming for. It may include the grade you are hoping to achieve (if known) and the purpose of your studies. It names the tutor you are working with and the kind of support that your tutor will be giving you. All these things may or may not be written down, but it is better that they are, so that you know exactly where you stand.

ACTIVITY 2

1. Design your own learning contract.
2. Include all the information you think is important.
3. Sign it, and ask someone you trust to countersign it.

4. Display your learning contract in the room in which you normally study.

B ORGANISING YOUR TIME

When to study

Once you have focused on your reasons for studying, you should plan your schedule. Your Study Plan is your key to getting organised. If you are motivated and organised you have a very good chance of success. This section looks in detail at how to design a Study Plan that you can implement without having to give up eating, sleeping, exercising, fulfilling your other obligations, or having fun.

The next section will look at *what* you intend to study. This section concentrates on *when* you are going to study. It's hard to generalise about how long particular courses take to complete. One advantage of studying at home is that you can work at your own pace. You don't have to be rushed by a teacher who wants to hurry through the syllabus without explaining it properly, or by fellow students who hold you up by asking questions to which you already know the answers.

How many hours to study?

Oxford Open Learning asks all new students to complete a Student Application Form, so by now you may well have filled one in yourself. One of the questions on this form asks 'How many hours each week will you be able to study?'

It's interesting to see how much study time different people believe they have available. Shefali Bhagat claims that she can spare 20 hours every week. As she has a full-time job, Shefali may find it hard to keep that up over a period of many months.

It's better to begin gently and build up to a more demanding timetable than start with an ambitious plan and disappoint yourself when you fall behind. Phillipa Kelly, who has a part-time job and two young children to look after, reckons that she will be able to find 5-10 hours per week for studying. Alan Carter, a private in the British Army, expects to study for 12-15 hours per week. He may find that this is more than he can manage.

Ibrahim Mahmoud doesn't specify a number of hours but instead writes that he will study for 'as many hours as it takes to pass'. Now, while this shows determination, it also shows that Ibrahim hasn't thought enough about how much time he will actually devote to his studies.

The estimates below offer a very rule-of-thumb guide to how many hours you may need to spend on your studies. They allow for a few weeks per year completely free of study, but you should remember that a regular routine is important. If you take too much holiday you will forget everything you've learned! You'll also find it hard to go back to your Study Plan. So bear these approximations in mind when you do Activity 3. The calculations assume at least 35 weeks of study per year:

- one GCSE may take a minimum of 6 hours per week for one year (35 weeks × 6 hours = 210 hours);

- one 'A' level may take a minimum of 10 hours per week for two years (70 weeks × 10 hours = 700 hours).

ACTIVITY 3

Here are some questions you need to answer before designing your Study Plan. You will need a blank Study Plan (several copies of this are enclosed in the document envelope that accompanies this *How to Study* guide). A calendar will also be useful. Write down your answers and keep them in your *How to Study: Activities* file.

1. On what date do you plan to take the exam?
2. What date is it now?
3. How many complete weeks are there between now and the exam?
4. Are there any weeks when you won't be able to study (e.g. holiday, job commitments?)
5. If so, subtract these weeks from the total.
6. How many weeks are left?
7. Look at the blank Study Plan.
8. Using a pencil (because you may need to make changes later) draw a line through any hours of the week when you will not be available for study. (You may be sleeping, working, playing sport, watching your favourite TV programmes, preparing food, looking for a new partner, cleaning your flat, etc.).
9. How many hours remain? These are potentially available for study. (If there are no hours left, or not enough, you will have to look again at the hours you have already allocated for other activities. For example, if you watch 15 hours TV every week, you may have to sacrifice some of your viewing time! By reducing 15 hours to eight, you will release seven hours for studying.
10. Now decide how many hours you *want* to study. Don't be over-ambitious: nobody can manage 50 hours per week,

especially with a job or a family to look after! You can always increase the amount of studying gradually, once you have established a pattern.

11. Choose from the available hours the most convenient times and mark these as study times. Try to spread your studying through the week. If you plan six hours per week, don't do all of this work on one day. A little studying often is much more effective than a single day-long session.

Of course, simply allocating time for study isn't enough. You also need to estimate how much time you will spend on each topic of the course and each lesson of your study pack.

Additionally, it is very helpful to keep a record of what you have achieved. If you regularly compare what you planned to do with what you achieved, your planning will become more accurate.

DESPERATE MEASURES!

Allow time for other activities

Most of us are busier than we think! You may need to reduce your leisure time, but don't cut it out altogether. And unless you've been spending your whole life in bed recently, don't aim to reduce your sleeping time significantly. (People's sleep requirements vary enormously: almost everybody needs at least five hours sleep, while few really need more than ten. About eight hours sleep per night is average.) Also allow sufficient time for preparing and eating healthy, regular, balanced meals.

Your Tutor-Marked Assignments

Now look at the column on the right of your Study Plan, headed 'TMA deadlines'. 'TMA' stands for 'Tutor-Marked Assignment'. TMAs are identified by letters of the alphabet (A, B, C, etc.). The number of TMAs will vary from course to course, but most will have about ten. For example, GCSE English Literature includes nine TMAs, (A-I).

How often you complete a TMA depends on how much time you devote to your studies, but you should not normally attempt more than one TMA per fortnight (one per month is about average).

ACTIVITY 4

1. As soon as you have finalised your Study Plan, choose dates when you will submit your TMAs.

2. Space them out fairly evenly, with the first assignment due about three or four weeks from now, and the last one due about two months before the examination.

3. There are two reasons for leaving time free of assignments at the end. One is that you will need to do

some revision and get some exam practice. The other reason is in case for some reason you have fallen behind with your TMA schedule.

4. Once you have filled in your Study Plan, together with your list of TMA deadlines, *stick to it.*

5. Send a copy to your tutor without delay, so that your tutor knows when to expect your TMAs.

6. If your Study Plan turns out not to be working, telephone your tutor to discuss it.

7. If you need to make significant changes to your Study Plan, send your tutor a copy of the revised version.

8. If you have problems with your Study Plan change it, but don't abandon it altogether. (See Chapter 4, Section A for more about you, your tutor, and your TMAs.)

Flexibility

Your Study Plan needs to be flexible. Your study pack is structured to include regular review of work completed. About two months before the exams, however, you should start to adapt your weekly Study Plan to allow for some time each week devoted to revision (see Section A of Chapter 6). Throughout your course, you should aim to include regular study, regular review, and regular practice of the new skills you have acquired.

Make use of available time

In this section, we've been talking about your management of time. While most of your studying should be done at the times specified in your Study Plan, and in a suitable environment (see Chapter 1, Section C), you should look for opportunities to make use of time that would otherwise be wasted. You won't be able to write an assignment on a bus journey, for example, but you may be able to do some background reading or plan an assignment.

Carry a notebook and pen around with you. You never know when you might have your next brilliant idea! Having a book to read also makes sense, just in case there's a queue in the bank or the post office.

Finally, here's proof that it's possible to achieve something during that 'dead' time, when most people sit doing nothing, or turning the pages of a magazine. I made the first draft of a plan for this book while on a long, boring bus journey from London to Birmingham. Time is precious: use it!

C GETTING TO KNOW YOUR COURSE

Find out about your syllabus

This section helps you to find out everything you need to know about your course of study.

As soon as possible, get hold of your syllabus and past exam papers. These will give you a clear picture of what you need to do in order to pass. If you are enrolled at your local college, your tutor may be able to provide these. Otherwise you can purchase them quite cheaply from the examination board. Payment for your syllabus and past papers should be by crossed cheque or postal order, made payable to the examination board. Don't send cash through the post.

An organisation like Oxford Open Learning cannot supply these documents because the examination boards hold the copyright to them. There are many different examining bodies in the UK, but Oxford Open Learning deals with only a few of these. Ensure that you request the correct syllabus and past papers from the correct examining body, giving the syllabus course code as well as the name of the subject. Always double-check these details before sending off your letter. Course codes for GCSE and 'A' level syllabuses appear in the Oxford Open Learning prospectus.

You should ensure that the syllabus you are using is up to date. All syllabuses are revised from time to time but some syllabuses change substantially every few years.

Register for the exams

If you are enrolled at your local college, it will be your examination centre. If you are studying directly through Oxford Open Learning, it is your job to find an examination centre. When you write to the examination board about your syllabus and exam papers, you can also ask about any nearby examination centres. You should also ask for the closing date for exam registration.

Oxford Open Learning strongly advises you to look for an examination centre at the earliest opportunity. If you are planning to write in June, you should start looking for a suitable exam centre early in December of the previous year. Your *last chance* to register for the June exams is in January of the same year. If you plan to write the January exams, you should register at a centre during August or September. The process takes time: don't leave it until it's too late! See Chapter 7, Section A for further details about enrolling for exams.

Write to your examining board

The relevant addresses for syllabuses, past exam papers, and information about exam centres and registration deadlines are as follows:

AEB & SEG
Stag Hill House
Guildford
Surrey
GU2 5XJ

☎ (01483) 506506

ULEAC
Stewart House
32 Russell Square
LONDON
WC1B 5DN

☎ (0171) 331 4000

NEAB
Devas Street
MANCHESTER
M15 6EX

☎ (0161) 953 1180

ACCA
29 Lincoln's Inn Fields
London
WC2A 3EE

☎ (0171) 396 5800

UCLES
1 Hills Road
CAMBRIDGE
CB1 2EU

☎ (01223) 553311

LCCI
Athena House
112 Station Road
Sidcup
Kent
DA15 7BJ

☎ (0181) 302 0261

Finding your way around the study pack

You will probably receive your study pack and start your course before you get your syllabus and past papers. Obviously, you should start at the beginning and work through the lessons in the correct sequence. But you should first read the introduction and *skim* through all the lessons to gain a rapid overview of the whole course (see Chapter 3, Section B).

ACTIVITY 5

Here are some questions about your study pack. Note down the answers and keep them in your *How to Study: Activities* file.

1. Where in the study pack is the structure of the course summarised?
2. Is the course divided into modules? If so, how many?
3. How many lessons are there altogether in the course?
4. Choose a module or section that looks interesting. Look at it for 15 minutes or so to get a clear picture of how it is structured. Write down any notable features or any questions to put to your tutor.
5. How many Self-Assessment Tests (SATs) are there in the module?
6. How many Tutor-Marked Assignments (TMAs) are there in the module?
7. How many TMAs are there in the whole course? (See Section C below.)
8. Read through Activity 7 below. Use the same method to assess your familiarity with, and interest in, the various modules in your study pack.
9. When you have received your syllabus and have examined it carefully, compare your answers to this activity with those in Activity 7.

Getting to know your syllabus

When the syllabus and past exam papers arrive, read through them carefully, marking any important details and anything that is unclear to you. If there is anything you do not understand, telephone your tutor for help (see Chapter 4, Section A). Do this immediately, while the problem is fresh in your mind!

ACTIVITY 6

Here are some important questions to ask about assessment. Write down the answers and file them in your *How to Study: Activities* file.

1. How many examination papers are there?
2. If there is more than one, how are the marks divided among the different papers?
3. How much time is allocated for each examination paper?
4. How many questions must you answer?
5. Are there any optional questions or sections in the examination paper?
6. If so, what are they?
7. Are marks divided equally among the questions?
8. If not, how many marks are available for each question?
9. What is the ratio between marks and minutes? (From this you can work out approximately how much time to spend on each question – see Chapter 6, Section C and Chapter 7, Section B for details).

10. What percentage of the total marks is allocated to the written examination paper(s)?

11. What percentage of the marks is allocated to coursework?

12. Exactly what coursework will you have to do?

13. What are the submission deadlines for coursework?

14. Are there any other requirements (e.g. oral, practicals?)

15. If so, how many marks are allocated for these?

16. Is it possible to do the exam in stages (for example, one module in January and another in June)?

17. If so, how often are you allowed to retake a module?

Some syllabuses offer two alternative routes to the qualification, known as *terminal* and *modular*. Most home learners (and Oxford Open Learning courses) aim for the terminal type of assessment.

Some syllabuses give information about how examiners will mark your work, such as a list of marking criteria. Look for such information in your syllabus. Later, you may be able to apply these criteria when reviewing your SATs (Self-Assessment Tests). If you know exactly what the examiners want, you are more likely to be able to give it to them.

How many hours of study?

Look for any indication of how many study hours, on average, are necessary to complete the course. These figures are always approximate, and the Oxford Open Learning way is to encourage you to study at a pace that is challenging but within reach, and this pace will be different for different people. It is nevertheless useful to have a rough idea of how much time you expect to spend on the whole course. This will make designing your Study Plan much easier (see Section B).

Study packs, textbooks and practicals

Generally, the study packs for GCSE subjects (Business Studies, Geography, or Economics, for example) contain everything you need to complete the course and prepare for the exam. However, at 'A' level, and in some GCSE subjects, such as Human Biology, you may need additional equipment and/or textbooks. You may also need to do some practical work.

In order to do practicals, you need to enrol at your local college. Oxford Open Learning is not in a position to arrange practicals for you. The prospectus uses a set of simple icons to show which courses have additional requirements.

It is always advisable to read as widely as possible in your subject. Even if your course is self-contained, you should make use of whatever additional resources are available, such as relevant textbooks or reference materials in your local library.

Explore your syllabus

When you know exactly how the assessment is organised, look at the syllabus in detail. Some topics may already be familiar, even if you have not studied them in depth. Other topics may be completely new to you. Think about each topic in turn. How familiar or unfamiliar is the topic? How interesting or boring does it seem? How difficult or easy do you think it will be?

The answers to many of these questions will probably be guesses, at least the first time you ask them. But there's no harm in forming an opinion based on limited information, as long as you are prepared to revise your opinion later.

If you review your progress regularly, your answers to these questions will gradually become more accurate. You may find it useful to do Activity 7 again when you launch your revision programme (see Sections A and B of Chapter 6). By then you should know where your weaknesses are and therefore where you need to focus your revision.

ACTIVITY 7

1. Make a list of the main headings or topics in the syllabus.
2. Look at each topic in turn.
3. Decide whether or not the topic is at all familiar.
4. If you already know a lot about the topic, write a number 1 next to it.
5. If you know absolutely nothing about it, give it a 5.
6. In this way, you can give each topic a 'familiarity grade' from 1 to 5.
7. Then decide how interesting or uninteresting each topic appears.
8. Give each topic a letter from A to E according to how interesting it looks, with A for the most exciting and E for topics that look utterly boring.
9. Each topic now has a number and a letter next to it. This code can help you to decide how much time and effort to put into different topics of your course. (Remember, though, it's only an estimate: you may need to revise your opinion later.)

If your list includes some 1s and 2s, or even 3s, it means that you already know *something* about the course you're studying. That's excellent news and should help with your self-confidence. You already possess some of the information and possibly some of the skills that you need in order to pass, so you're already one step ahead (see Chapter 1, Section A on self-image)!

If you have plenty of As, Bs and even some Cs, it means that you are already interested in some parts of the course. Again, you're winning!

If you have 4s and 5s (everybody will have some), it means that these parts of the course are new to you. Unless you've studied this course before, some or even most of the syllabus will consist of unfamiliar material. This is no problem, and the A1–E5 key is designed to help you to identify which parts of the course will need your closest attention. For example, if you grade a topic D4, D5, E4 or E5, you know immediately that this topic is likely to require much greater effort on your part than one which scored A1 or B2. Bear this in mind when designing your Study Plan and preparing for revision.

Problems with motivation

If you've given most of the topics on your course Ds and Es, you may have a motivation problem. Ask yourself what you can do to stimulate interest in at least some parts of the course. One answer may be to read (or re-read) Section A of this chapter and do (or re-do) Activity 1. You could also discuss the problem with your tutor.

If you really have no interest in the subject, you need to take a long hard look at why you are studying this course. If you can do without it, perhaps you should consider taking some other course that you find more interesting, although you should bear in mind that some key subjects are indispensable for certain career paths or types of employment. As a last resort, telephone your student adviser if you want to find out about changing courses, but don't forget that if you do change you will have to pay an administration fee!

D SARAH MOSS: A CASE STUDY

Introducing Sarah

This section revises some of the ideas we have dealt with so far in this book by making a case study of an Oxford Open Learning student called Sarah Moss. You may find it useful to compare Sarah's situation as a student to your own, noting any similarities and differences.

Sarah Moss is a thirty-two-year-old married woman who works full time as a sales assistant in a hardware store. Sarah's parents split up when she was nine, and as she was the eldest of four children, Sarah spent more time in her teenage years helping her mother to care for her two brothers and her baby sister than she did on her school work. Sarah was unemployed for the first four years after leaving school, but she eventually got a job as a sales assistant at Harry's Handy Hardware Store, and she has worked there ever since.

Sylvia Weston's plans

Last year Harry Hartnell sold up and retired, and the shop was taken over by a successful businesswoman, Sylvia Weston. Sylvia's intention from the beginning was to expand the business.

In July, Sylvia tells Sarah that there may be an opportunity for promotion next year. The business is going well, and she wants to open another branch in a neighbouring suburb. Sylvia plans to train Sarah to become assistant manager of the new branch.

When Sarah and Sylvia sit down to discuss this plan, Sylvia is surprised to find out how limited Sarah's qualifications are, and emphasises the need for accounting and business skills. Sarah admits that she doesn't have any formal qualification in either business or accounting, but feels she has the potential to do the job. She's learned a lot about business by working in the shop, but knows next to nothing about accounting. Sarah then decides to enquire about home-study courses.

Sarah contacts Oxford Open Learning

Sarah finds Oxford Open Learning in the Yellow Pages and gives them a call. She gets through to a student adviser called Norma, who tells Sarah about Oxford Open Learning's courses. Norma then sends Sarah the prospectus and an application form, which Sarah receives the next day.

Sarah shows the prospectus to Sylvia, pointing out the GCSE Accounting and Business Studies courses. Sylvia agrees that Sarah should enrol for these subjects. Sylvia adds that she is willing to spend a couple of hours a week giving Sarah some practical in-store training as preparation for her new post.

So Sarah sends off her completed application form, together with her first instalment. A couple of days later Sarah gets a call from Norma to discuss the details of her application. In particular, Norma wants to confirm the number of hours each week that Sarah plans to set aside for studying, and also when Sarah plans to sit her exams. Norma informs Sarah that she cannot be allocated to a tutor until her Study Plan has been agreed.

At this stage Sarah's estimate of time available for study is provisional. There will be time to make adjustments later if necessary. Norma asks Sarah to do Activity 3 of this chapter as soon as she receives her *How to Study* guide.

Norma then sends Sarah a copy of *How to Study at Home the Oxford Open Learning Way*, a standing order form and an enrolment form. The standing order form provides confirmation that Sarah's instalments will be paid regularly. The enrolment form enables Sarah to be allocated a tutor for each of her chosen subjects.

Sarah completes the standing order form and the enrolment form and sends them to Oxford Open Learning by return of post. She starts reading through the *How to Study* guide right away, as she eagerly awaits her study packs. Sarah decides to contact her exam board immediately. So she writes to the SEG to request syllabuses 3260

(Accounting) and 2660 (Business Studies) and some past exam papers.

Sarah receives her study packs

The study packs arrive a few days later. Sarah begins by spending about an hour on each of them. She doesn't read anything in detail but gets a general impression of the topics and how the lessons are structured. Then she starts to work through *How to Study at Home the Oxford Open Learning Way* and the opening lessons of both courses in more detail.

When the syllabuses arrive from SEG, Sarah spends several hours over a few days looking at them carefully, estimating the levels of familiarity and interest for each topic. So far, she hasn't completed any of the activities in the *How to Study* book, but now that she has her syllabuses in front of her, she decides to do Activity 7.

Sarah's Response to Activity 7

Accounting	Familiarity	Interest
Accounting data	4	B
Verification of accounting records	4	C
Development of the accounting model	4	C
Non-commercial organisations	5	B
Manufacturing concerns	5	D
Limited liability companies	5	E
Incomplete records	4	D
The analysis and interpretation of accounting statements	5	D

Business Studies	Familiarity	Interest
The business environment	2	C
Production and distribution	4	D
The market and marketing	4	A
Finance and accounting	5	D
Personnel	1	B
Communication and technology	3	B
Change and recent trends	4	C

ACTIVITY 8

Look carefully at Sarah's assessment of the topics in the two courses she wants to study. Think about these questions:

1. Which course does she know more about?
2. Which course appears to be of greater interest to her?
3. Which course do you think she will need to spend more time on? Why?

Sarah finds Activity 7 useful, so she decides to go back and do all the earlier activities in the *How to Study* book.

Sarah has had her study packs since the second week of August. Although it's too early to estimate how many hours of study time she will need to complete the course, Sarah has already agreed with Norma, her student adviser, that she plans to study for between 10 and 12 hours per week. She has also decided that she wants to take her exams in June next year.

Now Sarah wants to work out her Study Plan in more detail. She takes a blank copy and fills in times when she will be sleeping, commuting, working or busy around the house. She also sets aside time for rest and entertainment.

Sarah considers starting her day with an hour's studying (from 6.00 to 7.00 a.m.). But she doesn't like getting up early and she's worried about being late for work.

She wants to keep one day completely free of study. This is a good idea if you can manage it. She chooses Saturdays. But she discovers that if she keeps Saturdays free she will have to study on Friday evenings. After a busy working week, she is always tired on Fridays, so she doesn't think that's a good idea. Instead she pencils in some studying on Saturday, but keeps it down to only two hours.

She also decides to allocate more time to Accounting than to Business Studies, because her analysis of the topics has shown that she not only knows more about Business Studies, but is also more interested in this subject than in Accounting. She hopes, however, to develop an interest in accounts as she goes along.

Here are Sarah's responses to the first six questions in Activity 3:

1. Mid-June next year.
2. 13 August.
3. 43.
4. Yes: two weeks at Christmas and two weeks at Easter.
5. 43 – 4 = 39.
6. 35.

Sarah plans to allocate six hours per week to her Accounting course, and five to Business Studies. This makes a total of 11 hours per week. Sarah calculates that if she completes 11 hours study each week for the planned 39 weeks, she will spend a total of 39 × 11 = 429 hours on her courses. She remembers that the *How to Study* guide recommends a minimum of 200 hours per GCSE course, and notes that her plans allow her slightly more than 400 hours for her two GCSE subjects.

Here is Sarah's completed study timetable. It shows that Sarah will spend six hours per week studying Accounting (the periods marked 'A') and five hours per week on Business Studies (the periods marked 'B'). Sarah decided to go into more detail than you might want to about how she spends her time when she is *not* studying. For this reason Sarah invented a key, so that each hour of the Study Plan is labelled with a particular activity. I've reproduced her plan as she wrote it to give you a clear idea of exactly how she spends her time.

Sarah's key

A = Accounting study time

B = Business Studies study time

D = Domestic tasks (washing, ironing, cleaning)

E = Entertainment, including relaxation, hobbies, TV, etc.

G = Gym, exercise, sport

M = Meals (preparation and eating)

S = Sleep (including washing, getting dressed, etc.)

W = Work, including travel to and fro

Sarah's Study Plan

	Sun	Mon	Tue	Wed	Thu	Fri	Sat
6.00	S	S	S	S	S	S	S
7.00	S	M	M	M	M	M	S
8.00	S	W	W	W	W	W	S
9.00	M	W	W	W	W	W	S
10.00	A	W	W	W	W	W	G
11.00	B	W	W	W	W	W	G
12.00	D	W	W	W	W	W	A
1.00	D	M	M	M	M	M	B
2.00	M	W	W	W	W	W	M
3.00	D	W	W	W	W	W	D
4.00	D	W	W	W	W	W	D
5.00	D	W	W	W	W	W	D
6.00	D	G	G	G	G	G	E
7.00	E	M	M	M	M	M	E
8.00	M	A	B	A	B	A	M
9.00	E	A	B	E	E	E	E
10.00	S	S	S	S	S	S	E
11.00	S	S	S	S	S	S	E
12.00	S	S	S	S	S	S	S
1.00	S	S	S	S	S	S	S

The example below is a simplified version of Sarah's Study Plan. It shows only the times that Sarah has set aside for her studies. It's much easier to read than the version above. Study periods are marked with an A or B. All other times are left blank:

Sarah's Simplified Study Plan

	Sun	Mon	Tue	Wed	Thu	Fri	Sat
6.00							
7.00							
8.00							
9.00							
10.00	A						
11.00	B						
12.00							A
1.00							B
2.00							
3.00							
4.00							
5.00							
6.00							
7.00							
8.00		A	B	A	B	A	
9.00		A	B				
10.00							
11.00							
12.00							
1.00							

Although Sarah's estimates fit with Oxford Open Learning's guidelines, she doesn't yet know for sure whether she has set aside enough time for her studies. But by keeping a record each week of work accomplished (as well as a plan of what she *intends* to do) and by noting how long she spends on each lesson, she is soon able to adjust her timetable as necessary.

In fact, she finds that the Business Studies course is quite straightforward and that she can work through the material quickly. The Accounting course is a bit more interesting than she had expected, but it *is* difficult. She has to work through the first few lessons surprisingly slowly. So Sarah decides that she'll have to do some early morning study after all (from 6.00 to 7.00 on Monday mornings). This extra hour makes all the difference. Her Accounting course now keeps pace with her Business Studies.

A couple of weeks later Sarah discovers that she has got used to waking up earlier, and decides to get up at that time every weekday morning. She doesn't need any more study time at present, but by shifting her two hours of study on Saturdays to one hour each early on Tuesdays and Wednesdays, she is able to fulfil her original plan, which was to keep Saturdays completely free. So, four weeks after starting her home-study courses, Sarah revises her Study Plan. The revised version looks like this:

Sarah's Revised Study Plan

	Sun	Mon	Tue	Wed	Thu	Fri	Sat
6.00		A	B	A			
7.00							
8.00							
9.00							
10.00	A						
11.00	B						
12.00							
1.00							
2.00							
3.00							
4.00							
5.00							
6.00							
7.00							
8.00		A	B	A	B	A	
9.00		A	B				
10.00							
11.00							
12.00							
1.00							

3 IMPROVING YOUR STUDY SKILLS

A WHAT ARE STUDY SKILLS?

Study skills are simply the various skills you need to be able to study efficiently. Many people have surprisingly poor study skills. Merely attempting to learn facts and recite them like a parrot isn't enough. This chapter deals with how to improve your ability to study. It does this by identifying a number of skills and looking at them one at a time.

ACTIVITY 1

1. Spend 15 - 30 minutes reviewing Chapters 1 and 2 of this book.
2. Make a list of any skills mentioned that you think will help you to study more effectively.
3. Write down any other skills you know of that may be study skills.
4. As you read through the rest of Section A of this chapter, compare your list with the list of study skills given in the text.

Oxford Open Learning students have an advantage over students who are totally dependent on textbooks. This is because all Oxford Open Learning study packs offer advice on how to develop your study skills. This advice is accompanied by activities tailored to the subject you are working on. This ensures that if you work through the activities carefully you will become more familiar with the topics of your course, and also improve your study skills.

Here is an example. The first module of the 'A' level Biology study pack is called 'Levels of Organisation'. This module focuses on a particular study skill (see *Classification* below) which forms one of the cornerstones of Biology. Classification depends on comparing and contrasting items. If you don't know how to compare and contrast ideas, objects, or organisms, you won't be able to develop a system for classifying them.

Not every subject requires exactly the same techniques, but we can identify a list of core skills that are common to most subjects. Without these skills successful study would be difficult or impossible. I have arranged them into two groups, headed *Receptive Skills* and *Productive Skills*, although there is some overlap between the two categories.

Receptive skills

- skimming
- scanning
- using abbreviations
- making notes
- taking notes
- summarising
- understanding classification
- recognising different kinds of text
- reference skills
- using the media in a discerning way

Productive skills

- brainstorming, mind-maps and planning an assignment
- breaking up large tasks into smaller units
- recycling your studies

- solving problems
- improving your memory
- making inferences
- translating information from one form into another
- empathising
- assessing your own progress

ACTIVITY 2

1. What do the two terms *receptive* and *productive* mean?
2. If you don't know the answer, how can you find out?
3. What do you think is the main difference between *receptive* and *productive* skills?
4. Can you identify any overlaps between the two lists above?
5. In other words, which of the above skills involve both receptive and productive aspects?

B RECEPTIVE STUDY SKILLS

These skills are largely *receptive* skills. That is, they deal with acquiring and processing new information.

Skimming

Skimming consists of reading rapidly to get an overview; when skimming you don't read every word. Instead you look at introductory pages, titles, headings and any pictures or diagrams for clues about the contents and how the text is structured. You might glance at parts of the main text but would not read it in detail (see Chapter 2, Section C).

ACTIVITY 3

You need a newspaper that you have not looked at, or an old one that you have not read recently. You also need a watch or clock.

Read the instructions below before you begin. Don't worry if this activity seems difficult. Most people do not absorb information quickly, which is why we need to practise skimming. For example, I just spent five minutes skimming a page from *The Oxford Times*. Of 12 news stories, I could only recall a few words about each of four of them. The rest were a complete blank!

1. Open the newspaper at a page on which there are several news stories.
2. Spend exactly five minutes *skimming* this page.
3. Do not write anything down yet.
4. During this time, read the headlines and look at any accompanying photos.
5. Briefly look at any other illustrations or additional material on the page.
6. Next, *skim* through the articles looking for key words. (This means looking quickly down the columns of print.)
7. Remember: you will not have time to read any of the articles in detail.
8. After exactly five minutes, close the newspaper so that you cannot see the page you have been skimming. (There's no point in cheating. This is not a test!)

9. Now answer the questions numbered 10-13 below. Don't worry if you can't remember much.
10. How many articles appeared on the newspaper page?
11. Write no more than five words about each article.
12. Write brief notes on any photos you noticed.
13. What else was on the page besides news articles and press photos?
14. Now open the newspaper page again and check how you did.

If you're as bad as I am at this skill, you'll need plenty of practice. Try Activity 3 every day for a week, using different texts, and you will improve. The skill of skimming is related to skills such as *summarising* and *improving your memory*, so you could also check the information on summarising and improving your memory below.

ACTIVITY 4

1. Skim through Chapter 5 of this book. Allow yourself exactly five minutes to do this.
2. Without referring back to the text, what is Chapter 5 about?
3. How many sections is Chapter 5 divided into?
4. What is the topic of each section?
5. How many activities are there in Chapter 5?
6. Which section do you think will be most useful to you?

7. Why?

8. Check back to Chapter 5. If you were unable to answer the questions correctly, do the same activity for Chapter 6.

Scanning

Unlike skimming, which provides an overview of a text, scanning sets out to look for specific details. For example, if you wanted to buy a second-hand car, you would *scan* the relevant column of your local paper. Scanning means looking quickly at a lot of text in search of *particular* information.

ACTIVITY 5

1. Find the television page for any weekday in any newspaper.

2. Look for the five main national broadcasters.

3. Don't bother about satellite or cable TV.

4. Spend exactly two minutes *scanning* the listings, looking for all sports programmes

5. Afterwards, go back to see if you missed any.

6. If you want further practice, try the same exercise with a different day's TV page. This time, scan for movies.

Using abbreviations

Several study skills depend upon the ability to use abbreviations effectively. When *making* notes (from a text in front of you), abbreviations help you to summarise information in a small space. This is immensely useful when you start your revision programme.

When *taking* notes (while listening to someone speaking), abbreviations are even more useful. Some students try to write down everything the lecturer or broadcaster is saying. This is impossible! These days few people learn shorthand (if you do know shorthand, use it!), so we need to use abbreviations. Many of these are standard, but you will find it helpful to invent your own. Here is a list of well-established abbreviations:

alt.	alternative
approx.	approximately
a.s.a.p.	as soon as possible
C	century
c.	approximately
cd	could
cf.	compare
cont'd	continued
exc.	except
e.g.	for example
esp.	especially
et al.	and others
et seq.	and what follows
ff.	following pages
fr.	from
ibid.	in the same work as quoted above
inc.	including
i.e.	that is

info	information
i.r.o.	in respect of
no.	number
op. cit.	in the work quoted
opp.	opposite
p.	page
pp.	pages
q.v.	see
re:	with reference to
shd	should
usu.	usually
v.	very
vs	against
viz.	namely
wd	would
wh.	which
w/o	without
yr	your
+	and
&	and
=	equals
≠	doesn't equal
<	less than
>	more than
//	parallel, similar or equivalent to
∴	therefore
∵	because
≅	approximately equal to
→	it follows that
←	results from, depends upon
#	space

Acronyms such as BBC, UFO, UNESCO are also useful abbreviations. When writing history notes, for example, it is quicker to write 'WW2' than 'World War 2' or 'The Second World War'. Some dictionaries include lists of common acronyms and abbreviations.

Making notes

By *making notes* I'm referring to writing notes on what you are reading. Notes are a way of summarising information and a way of remembering it. Notes are not complete sentences, but words, phrases and abbreviations, usually arranged as a list. Your notes are mainly for *your* benefit, not for other people's, and are therefore a personal matter.

Your notes should, however, be clearly written and easy to make sense of later. There may be a gap of weeks or months between making notes and referring to them. So it's best to leave plenty of space around your pages of notes to make them easy to read.

The study skill *making notes* is closely connected with the following study skills (see below): taking notes, using abbreviations, summarising, improving your memory.

ACTIVITY 6

This activity asks you to compare the note-making skills of three Oxford Open Learning students, and then decide which notes are the most effective.

1. First, read through the following short extract, entitled 'The Product Life Cycle', which is taken from the GCSE Business Studies study pack, Module 2, Lesson 8. The notes that follow are based on this extract:

Marketing executives tend to think of products and particular brands as though they had a life of their own. It is as if they are born, go through various stages similar to those of human development, and eventually die.

As babies and small children, we require a great deal of looking after and we cannot repay the investment that is put into us. It is the same with a new product. A great deal of money must be spent in research, product development, and initial advertising before the business begins to see a return on its investment. When the product reaches its intended market, there will be a period (like an apprenticeship, perhaps) when costs are balanced by revenue and eventually, when the product is established, it should make a profit. Now that it is "mature", it can support other developing products.

But its earning power will not last for ever. One day no one will want to buy it any more and it would be a waste of money to continue advertising it. So, in its "old age", the product may still be available but it is no longer actively promoted. Eventually, it must be withdrawn altogether.

It is important to know where abouts a product is in its life cycle. This will have an effect on the amount of promotion that is organised and perhaps also on the planning of production. There is no use building a bigger factory if a product's sales are just about to go into an unavoidable decline.

2. Now look closely at the note-making attempts of the three students:

Michelle's notes

Mkt execs think of prods + brands as if alive.
// human: born → devel → die.

Babies req. much attn + can't repay investment.
// new prod: £££ spent on research, devel + ads.
next period // apprentshp when costs = revenue.
→ mature prod → profit + supp other devel
prods.

Next period = prod's old age. Few or no more
sales.
No pt adv old prod.
Final stage: prod withdrawn.
Must know where each prod is in life cycle.
→ amt of promo + production plans.
No pt bldg bigger factory for prod abt to decline.

Daniel's notes

Me think ps and pbs as though life of own
Bn dev die.

As b.s + sms, we req gt dl lkg aft and we
cant rpy invt pt into us.
Same new p. Gt dl mny mst spt rsch p dev
and in ad b b b see rtn on in.

When p rch mkt, p like app costs bal rev +
even when est shd make p.
Now mat can supp oth dev ps.

Earn pow nt 1st frev
One day no one wnt buy it. Wst mny cont ad it.

Old age p ava but no lng act p. Evnt w/drawn alt.

Imp knw where p is in life cyc. Efct amt p org + p
onp + p.

No use bldg bgr fctry if ps sls abt to go into
unavd decl.

Sarah's notes

product // life: birth → death

a) new prod: costs, no return

b) 'apprenticeship': costs = revenue

c) 'mature': profit

d) prod. 'dies': no profit – withdraw

need to know where prod. is in life cycle

3. How easy or difficult is each set of notes to understand?
4. How concise is each set of notes?
5. Now read the extract again.
6. Look through the three sets of notes again.
7. Think about the differences among them.
8. Which set of notes is the most effective, and why?

ACTIVITY 7

1. Choose any page from your study pack that you have not yet studied in detail.
2. It's a good idea to choose a page from the module that you are currently studying.
3. The page should be all or mostly text.
4. The page should also be as self-contained, i.e. as complete in itself, as possible.
5. Read through the page carefully.
6. Make notes from the page, being as brief as possible, without omitting any of the main points.

7. Make sure any abbreviations are clear and unambiguous.
8. When you have finished, close your study pack so that you cannot see the page from which you have made notes.
9. Now try to write out the page based on your notes.
10. When you have done this, open the study pack again.
11. Check your attempt against the original page of the study pack.

It doesn't matter if your phrasing is different from the original, but check carefully that you have covered the main points.

Taking notes

In this book we distinguish between *making* notes and *taking* notes. Here, *making* notes means writing notes from written information: you have a book or study pack in front of you, and you have time to refer back to the text if you need to.

The phrase *taking* notes, on the other hand, means writing notes as you listen to someone speaking. This may be in a 'live' lecture or class, or while listening to a radio programme or watching TV. You may also need to write down points while someone (such as your tutor) speaks to you on the telephone.

While *making* notes is a relatively leisurely activity, *taking* notes is more pressured, because there is usually no opportunity to listen to the information again (unless you are listening to a recording). Taking notes is therefore more difficult than making notes, requiring you to listen for relevance and summarise what you hear *as* you write it down.

ACTIVITY 8

You need a radio cassette recorder (or a video recorder) for this activity. You also need a suitable cassette with at least ten minutes of blank tape. If you don't have a radio cassette player or a video recorder, try the alternative version of this activity below. Read all the instructions before you start.

1. Tune in to a radio or television station a few minutes before a news broadcast. (Choose another kind of programme if you want to, but it must be information-based. A documentary would be suitable, but *Top of the Pops* would not.)

2. The broadcast should be at least five minutes long.

3. Start recording about a minute before the broadcast is due to begin.

4. Sit comfortably with pen and paper and take notes.

5. Do not try to write down everything: include only the main points.

6. Use your abbreviation skills as practised above.

7. When the broadcast is over, stop the tape.

8. Look at your notes while they are still fresh in your mind. Make any changes or additions you want to.

9. Rewind the tape to the beginning of the broadcast.

10. Play back the recording, checking your notes as you go along.

11. Press the pause button if you need to stop and think about anything.

If you are not happy about your note-taking skills, try this activity again, using a different broadcast.

ACTIVITY 8 (ALTERNATIVE VERSION)

1. Follow the instructions for the activity above, but instead of using a tape or video machine, ask someone to help you.

2. Ask the person to read aloud a news story from a newspaper, or a page from your study pack, or textbook.

3. The material should be unfamiliar to you.

4. The person should read clearly and at a normal speaking speed, as if giving a lecture or reading the news.

5. Do not interrupt their reading.

6. While the person is speaking, take notes, using the skills you have practised under *Using abbreviations* and *Making notes* above.

7. When the person has finished speaking, allow yourself a few minutes to check your notes. Add any details you think are important and clarify what you have already written.

8. Now look at the reading text.

9. Compare the text with your notes.

If you don't feel that you are very good at note-taking, try the activity again a day or two later, using a different text

---

Summarising

The skills you have been practising in this chapter are useful when *summarising*. Indeed, notes are a form of summary. Most of your efforts to record information should be in note form. Sometimes, however, you will need to write up a summary in complete sentences. Some syllabuses formally test this skill in the examination.

In coursework assignments or project work, you may have to summarise the results of an experiment, the arguments of a thinker, or perhaps the plot of a novel.

ACTIVITY 9

This informal activity practises a combination of *Using abbreviations*, *Taking notes* and *Summarising*.

1. Take notes on the main events of an episode of your favourite soap opera, drama series or situation comedy.
2. Do this while the show is being broadcast.
3. When the show is over, work your notes up into a summary.

Recognising different kinds of text

This is a question of what language is appropriate in a particular situation. Sometimes it's just a question of which words to choose. 'Your company is requested at...' and 'Please come to a party at...' mean more-or-less the same thing, but they are used on quite different occasions. The first is formal, and uses a passive verb. The second is informal, and uses an active verb.

Science generally prefers the passive voice, because it suggests formality and objectivity. If you say 'We did this' and 'We did that', it implies that someone else might have done it differently. But phrases like 'This was done' and 'That was done' imply that you followed an agreed procedure, and that any experimenter would have done the experiment in the same way.

Look at these examples of highly *inappropriate* use of language:

Dear Mr Higginbottom,

re: the intimacy of our relationship

I am writing to inform you that my feelings towards you have recently become more serious. I therefore request your company next Friday evening. I have purchased two tickets for the 9.00 showing of "Titanic" at the local Astoria cinema. Please inform me in writing not later than Tuesday as to whether or not you will be available.

I look forward to seeing you.

Yours sincerely,

Helen Simpson.

Dear Phil

I just can't cope with my overdraft limit. I need to borrow much more money. I'd be really chuffed if you could dig into your pockets and come up with another five grand or so, otherwise me and my family will never make it through till Christmas.

Thanks a lot.

Love

Bobby

A science report.

Last Tuesday Joanne and I took a bottle of distilled water and threw a whole load of salt into it. Then we stirred it up with a small thing a bit like a spoon. We had to heat the water up for a while to get all the salt to dissolve. Then we heated the water more strongly until it started to boil. In fact, we carried on boiling the water until we could see some of the salt again. Eventually all the water boiled away and we were left with just the salt. Oh, I forgot to mention that at the end of the boiling process we had to slow down the heating to avoid burning the salt. That's all!!

ACTIVITY 10

Choose any one of the three examples on pages 77 and 78 and rewrite it in more suitable language.

Reference skills

Reference skills include the ability to use the following:

- chapter headings
- contents pages
- database
- dictionary
- encyclopaedia
- index
- library catalogue
- thesaurus

It's essential that you can use all these items. The Internet also offers millions of pages of information, available to anyone who has access to the worldwide web.

You also need to be able to use a library. If you want help, ask a librarian. That's what they are employed for: to help the public, especially students.

Most public libraries in the UK are well organised and staffed by competent, helpful librarians. They should be able to tell you everything you need to know about your library.

If you go to your library to look for a specific book, don't necessarily expect to find it immediately. The book may have been borrowed, in which case you will have to reserve it. Or it may only be available on inter-library loan from another library. It may then be a week or two before the book you need is in your hands.

For these reasons, *never* leave your library visits until the day before your assignment is due. You should *always* identify the information you need early on, at the planning stage. Make your enquiries at the library with plenty of time to spare.

ACTIVITY 11

1. Choose any author, book, topic or key word with which you are having difficulty.
2. Go to your library and use all available means to find out everything you can about your chosen author or topic in one hour.

Ask a librarian to help you if necessary.

Using the media

This skill is a reference skill. We are bombarded with information all day long - on TV, on the radio, on our way to work. How do we sort out the useful from the useless?

You might think this is easy. If you like beer, you'll pay attention to ads for beer and ignore the others. If you're a chocolate addict, you'll respond to chocolate ads. But there is simply so much information firing at us from all sides, that we get overloaded. We need to filter out the useless information without blunting our senses altogether. Otherwise we will miss some of the useful information too.

Here's an example. Recently I was thinking about the subsection below on *Improving your memory*. So far I had only scribbled a few notes. Then it was lunchtime.

The local Midlands news was on TV. I wasn't paying attention because I was still thinking about memory. Then I noticed that the news story was about a man who had an excellent memory! Of course, I started listening, but I'd already missed the beginning of the story.

The man was a Midlands taxi driver who could remember vast amounts of information. I'll tell you more about his technique under *Improving your memory* below. For now, the point is this. I had decided not to listen to the news, thinking it wouldn't be relevant. Because of that, I'd almost missed a chance to learn something new that could enrich my work.

There's plenty of educational material on radio and TV if you look for it. Last night I watched a fascinating Open University programme about the Romans in Britain. At the end the narrator offered a free information pack to anyone who wrote to the address given or telephoned a freephone number. It's worth being aware of such opportunities to supplement your studies!

Most educational programmes are transmitted during the night. Although suitable for all students, they are particularly good news for home learners, as they keep you in touch with the world beyond your study pack.

You would be well-advised to get in the habit of checking the TV listings every day and videotaping any programmes that look as though they might be relevant. You can tape over such programmes once you have viewed or skimmed through them. Of course, if you don't have access to a VCR, you may have to stay up late to watch relevant programmes at the time of broadcast, but this is not really to be recommended.

ACTIVITY 12

1. Get an up to date magazine or weekend newspaper which lists a whole week of TV and radio programmes.
2. Look carefully through the programme listings.
3. Mark programmes that look relevant to your studies.
4. Watch or listen to as many of these programmes as you can, making notes on their usefulness.
5. *Scan* the paper for articles relevant to your subject.

ACTIVITY 13

Go to your newsagent and look for any publications that are relevant to your studies. Make a note of the titles. Look for these in your library.

ACTIVITY 14

Go to your local library and find an educational video or audio cassette that is relevant to your subject of study.

C PRODUCTIVE STUDY SKILLS

Productive skills deal with how you plan and present your own ideas, based on information that you have already worked through.

Brain-storming, mind-maps and planning an assignment

Mind-maps and *spider diagrams* are names for two techniques that are very similar. To *save* space I will refer to *mind-maps* only from now on.

Brainstorming is what happens immediately before you produce a mind-map. As the name suggests, brainstorming is creative (often chaotic) thinking. For many people, mind-maps are the best way of getting the brainstorm down on paper.

Ideas do not usually arrive fully-formed or in the best sequence. Some people lose their moments of genius because the ideas they have don't seem to fit into their plan. But at the beginning it's best to scribble down whatever comes into your head, as long as it has *some* relevance to the topic.

Spread your ideas out over the page, using lines or arrows to make connections. Because mind-maps are arranged *spatially* instead of in a *linear* way, the links between ideas are not final. You can always rearrange the order, or the emphasis, later.

Page 86 shows an example of a mind-map made during a brainstorming session. The example topic is a GCSE English question on Shakespeare's play, *Macbeth*: "To what extent is Macbeth responsible for his own downfall?"

(Note that normally a literary essay must include clear references to the text in question. To save space, I have omitted these here.)

Once you have a mind-map in which the connections among ideas are clearly shown, you can begin to *plan* your essay. This involves restructuring your notes in a *linear* way, so that your ideas are presented in a suitable sequence. Generally, you would open with an introductory paragraph and end with a conclusion, which sums up what you have argued.

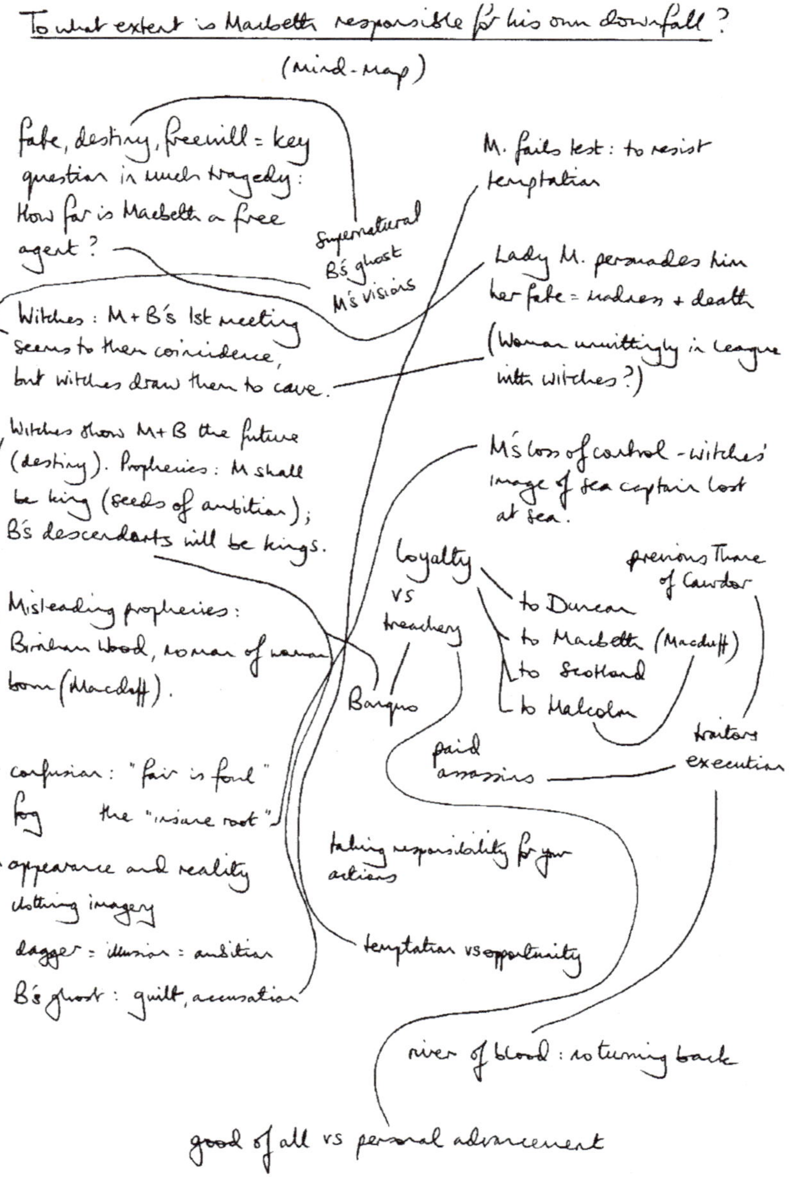
To what extent is Macbeth responsible for his own downfall?
(mind-map)
fate, destiny, freewill = key question in much tragedy: How far is Macbeth a free agent?
Supernatural
B's ghost
M's visions
M. fails test: to resist temptation
Lady M. persuades him
her fate = madness + death
Witches: M + B's 1st meeting seems to them coincidence, but witches draw them to cave.
(Woman unwittingly in league with witches?)
Witches show M + B the future (destiny). Prophecies: M shall be king (seeds of ambition); B's descendants will be kings.
M's loss of control - witches' image of sea captain lost at sea.
loyalty
vs
treachery
to Duncan
to Macbeth (Macduff)
to Scotland
to Malcolm
previous Thane of Cawdor
Misleading prophecies: Birnam Wood, no man of woman born (Macduff).
Banquo
traitors
paid assassins
execution
confusion: "fair is foul"
fog
the "insane root"
appearance and reality
clothing imagery
dagger = illusion = ambition
B's ghost: guilt, accusation
taking responsibility for your actions
temptation vs opportunity
river of blood: no turning back
good of all vs personal advancement

ACTIVITY 15

1. Choose a topic that you have already studied but have not yet written about.
2. Brainstorm your ideas.
3. Write down anything you think is relevant, spreading your ideas over the page.
4. Look at your notes and draw lines connecting any ideas that are related.
5. Finally, set out your notes in a linear way in the order in which you want to present them.
6. Write the assignment based on your plan.

Breaking up large tasks into smaller units

We looked at this skill briefly in Chapters 1 and 2. You can apply it to any situation in which a big, daunting task is worrying you. Simply divide the task into smaller units and tackle the problem a piece at a time. Spread the units of work over a period of hours, days or weeks, depending on the time scale. Build these sessions into your regular study plan.

This skill is useful if you have to write a long assignment for your coursework, or if you need to schedule a project over several weeks or months. I've used it extensively when planning this book.

Your studies are already organised for you into manageable units. Your syllabus is divided into topics and sub-topics. And a good home study pack will be structured so that you can work through it lesson by lesson, at your own pace. Self-assessment tests (SATs) and tutor-marked assignments (TMAs) are placed at intervals throughout the course to enable you and your tutor to measure your progress with confidence and accuracy.

ACTIVITY 16

7. Imagine you have won the National Lottery.
8. You decide to buy a plot of land where you will design and build your dream home.
9. Obviously, you can't do this overnight.
10. List the steps you will take to see this project through, from the first idea to the finished home.

Recycling your studies

Don't bore yourself to death with endless repetition. There are better ways of remembering one section of your studies when you proceed to the next. Build into your study plan regular opportunities to review your work. The aim is to renew your interest and clarify your understanding, not kill off both altogether.

Syllabuses tend to start with the simpler material and move on to the more advanced. But this applies more to some subjects that others. Science subjects and foreign languages, for example, tend to advance in complexity from one topic to another, whereas subjects such as History or Law may deal with a range of related topics of more-or-less equal difficulty.

From the beginning, build some time into your Study Plan to allow you to develop the skill of *recycling* (see Section C of Chapter 2, and Chapter 5).

ACTIVITY 17

1. Choose a topic that you studied some time ago, preferably one that you cannot remember much about.
2. Carefully read through your notes on this topic.
3. Spend half an hour skimming through the course material that relates to the topic.
4. Decide which parts of this topic need the most revision (see Chapter 2, Section C).
5. Build your revision of this topic into your Study Plan over the next two weeks (see Chapter 2, Section B).

Solving problems

We all need problem-solving skills regardless of what subjects we are studying, and even if we are not studying at all. This is especially true of problems for which we are unprepared and which therefore require creative solutions.

The most efficient problem-solvers use techniques such as brainstorming and *lateral thinking* to tackle new situations. Edward de Bono (who introduced the term *lateral thinking*) also suggested the term *provocation* as a way of jolting our minds into seeing problems in a new way. These approaches give us the freedom to take a new idea and see where it goes.

New ideas often get a hostile reception at first. The person who invented the safety razor was ridiculed by the so-called experts. They said the metal he wanted to use would break because it was too thin. But he went ahead and made the razor anyway, and now nobody uses the old-style cut-throat razor, which was as dangerous as its name suggests!

In a recent radio interview, Edward de Bono gave an example of *provocation* as a way of *opening up* a problem.

The problem was as follows. Factories that require a lot of water for their processes are often built near a river. They draw clean water from upstream, and pump polluted water back into the river downstream of the site. How can we prevent factories from polluting our rivers?

The government could pass strict laws, but some factories may ignore them, and monitoring factories may be expensive. Is there any way of persuading factories to monitor their own water usage, and thus reduce levels of pollution? (Try comparing the two diagrams on page 91.)

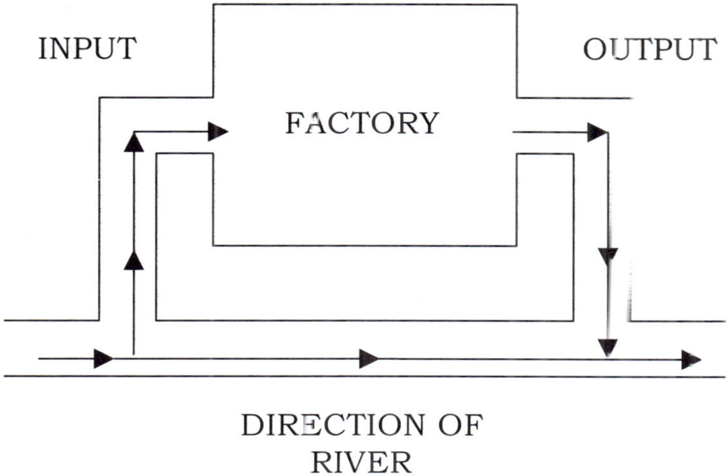
INPUT
OUTPUT
FACTORY
DIRECTION OF
RIVER

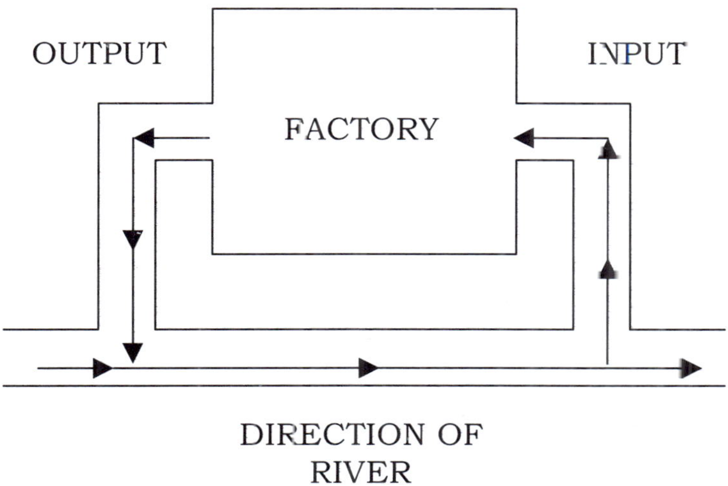
OUTPUT
INPUT
FACTORY
DIRECTION OF
RIVER

Here de Bono introduces his provocation, which is this apparently nonsensical statement: to persuade the factory to control water pollution, the factory must be *downstream of itself*. How can a factory be downstream of itself? Surely this is impossible!

Not at all: you can insist that the factory simply reverses its points of input and output. In other words, it pumps the water it needs from downstream, and returns to the river the water it has used *upstream* of itself.

Assuming that the factory needs a source of clean water to run its processes, this arrangement will force the factory to regulate its own water usage, thus minimising pollution. The solution is remarkably simple.

To sum up, most thinking occurs within an established frame of reference. We need a frame of reference to be able to think at all. But sometimes we miss possibilities because our view of things is too narrow. Lateral thinking allows us to step outside the frame and see things from a fresh perspective.

Improving your memory

There are many ways of doing this, such as using mnemonics, visualisation, and narratisation. You can also use symbols, charts and diagrams. Most of us make little use of our memory. A lot of research has been conducted into memory over the past few decades. It is now well established that developing your memory is largely a question of training.

Let's look at mnemonics first. A mnemonic is a way of making information memorable by turning initials into a kind of story. Some examples are probably familiar to you. If you want to remember the colours of the rainbow, you may have learned the sentence 'Richard of York gave battle in vain.' The first letter of each word represents a colour in the sequence:

R	red
O	orange
Y	yellow
G	green
B	blue
I	indigo
V	violet

It doesn't matter how ridiculous a mnemonic is: in fact, the silliness makes it easier to remember. It just occurred to me that 'mnemonic' is a difficult word to spell. So here's a mnemonic to remember how to spell the word 'mnemonic':

> 'Most neurologists eat marshmallow or nougat in Croydon.'

ACTIVITY 18

1. Find three words that you often have difficulty spelling correctly.
2. Invent a mnemonic for each of them.

I'm hopeless at remembering numbers. This is how I learned my car registration number, which is J611 UVC. J happens to be the first letter of my surname (Johnson). The number 611 is like the American emergency number 911, but with the 9 upside down. UV is a standard abbreviation for 'ultra-violet'. And C stands for 'car'!

This probably sounds ridiculous, but I repeat, the more ridiculous, the easier a mnemonic is to remember. It doesn't matter either that my car is actually red, as long as I remember the correct number. If I want to recall my registration number I say to myself: 'Johnson 611, ultra-violet car.'

Visualisation involves placing information spatially in your imagination. Let's suppose that you are studying Chemistry. You want to memorise the periodic table. You could take different sections of the table and, in your imagination, 'place' each section in a different room of your home. Or if you are studying English, you could take the plot of a novel and think of it as a journey along the street in which you live.

Another way to improve your memory is to write information down and then copy it out again. But beware of *passive* copying. Your brain may go to sleep while your hand mechanically copies out the text!

If you have a tape recorder with a microphone, you could read your notes onto a tape and play back the tape to yourself from time to time. While revising for a literature exam, a friend of mine played a tape recording of Shakespeare's play *Hamlet* back to herself every night for a week, while she was asleep! This might sound like a thoroughly *passive* thing to do, but the brain is actually quite receptive to external sounds and other sensations as we sleep.

Diagrams, pictures and flow charts can be good ways of remembering information, especially if you brighten them up by using a system of colour-coding.

ACTIVITY 19

1. Look at the introduction to your Oxford Open Learning study pack.
2. Find the heading 'The Content of the Course'.
3. Devise a diagram to summarise the course content.
4. Make sure you include the title of each module and lesson.
5. How can you colour-code your diagram to assist your memory?

Symbols are a great way of concentrating a lot of information into a small space. Road traffic signs are a good example. Drivers wouldn't have time to read a set of long-winded instructions, but by learning a few simple symbols they are able to understand quite complex information at a glance.

Many textbooks use symbols, or icons, to identify particular activities or themes. You can invent your own symbols to help you to remember key facts and ideas.

Understanding classification

Classification is more important in some subjects than in others, but it has some relevance to all of them. Biology, for example, is hugely dependent on classification.

Language itself is a system of classification. Sometimes objects or ideas can be classified in different ways.

Here's a simple example of classification. Look at this list of objects.

- ruler
- pencil
- pen
- thermometer
- rain gauge
- marker pen
- stick of chalk
- tape measure

This list can be divided into two categories: instruments of writing and drawing, and instruments of measurement:

writing and drawing	measurement
pencil	thermometer
pen	rain gauge
marker pen	ruler
stick of chalk	tape measure

ACTIVITY 20

Classify this list of items according to what they are made of. (If the item is made of more than one material, choose the material it is mostly or usually made of.)

window	violin	table
computer disk	wine glass	tape cassette
light bulb	knife	telephone
scissors	cricket stump	lawnmower
paper clip	pencil	teaspoon

Making inferences

To *infer* is to make an educated guess. Some people won't admit they make guesses, but if your guesses are based on all the evidence available, they are often the best you can do. And if you're studying English or another language, you will find yourself making inferences all the time.

Every time you see an unfamiliar word you need to work out what it means from its context. If you lack the courage to make inferences, you will miss valuable learning opportunities.

ACTIVITY 21

Below is a paragraph from a story. Some of the words have been replaced by nonsense words. These are highlighted in bold.

1. Read the paragraph and *infer* the meaning of the nonsense words.

2. Replace the nonsense words with suitable real words.

   The building was so ***lerp*** *that it seemed to pierce the sky. Helen looked* ***ek*** *at it from the street. She walked towards the* ***glot*** *and went inside. As she was going to the 12th* ***dumble****, she decided not to walk up the* ***hiddles****. She pressed the button to summon the lift instead. The lift travelled so* ***ratly*** *that it only took a few seconds to* ***crend*** *the 12th **dumble**. Helen knocked on the **glot** of office 1202. A **tarbow** inside called 'Come in!'*

Translating information from one form into another

This skill is formally tested in some subjects, such as Geography, where you might be asked to describe in words certain features of a landscape after interpreting symbols on a map. The ability to translate information from one form to another also plays a major role in enabling you to take an *active* role in your revision (see Chapter 6).

ACTIVITY 22

1. This activity asks you to draw a graph on a sheet of graph paper.
2. The graph will record the daily maximum temperature in Birmingham during a one-week period in December.
3. All the information you need to draw your graph appears in the following paragraph:

   On Monday 14 December the highest daytime temperature was surprisingly warm: 11°C, in fact. The next day it dropped to 4°C. On Wednesday 16 December the maximum temperature was only 2°C. Thursday saw a daytime high of 7°C, and the next day was 3°C warmer. The temperature cooled by 4°C on Saturday and the maximum temperature on Sunday was the same.

4. When you have finished, note how much more concise (and therefore easier to remember) your graph is than the paragraph of information.

Empathising

Empathy involves attempting to put yourself into the position of another. It is an imaginative way of escaping from our subjectivity, i.e. from seeing things only from our own, personal, limited point of view.

The skill of empathising is useful in the study of History, where we might want to imagine what it was like, for example, to be a peasant during the Russian Revolution. It is also important in English Literature, where we might imagine how it felt to be Banquo in Shakespeare's *Macbeth*. Indeed, history syllabuses often ask students to empathise with people caught up in specific historical situations.

But scientists use empathy too. The other day I heard a radio programme about evolution. One expert talked about how he had found it useful to try to imagine what it's like to be a gene!

More commonly, empathy is useful when simply trying to understand another person's point of view. We try to solve conflicts by discussion and negotiation rather than by going to war. We are not always successful in this, but empathy surely plays a major role in our efforts.

ACTIVITY 23

1. Choose one of the following and try to imagine what it would be like to be this person or thing.

2. Write a paragraph describing how you feel in your imagined identity.

- Claudia Schiffer
- Tony Blair on the day he won the 1997 General Election
- your next-door neighbour

- a £2 coin
- a molecule of water
- a squirrel coming out of hibernation in the spring
- a computer
- a dog whose owners are kind but do not notice how intelligent it is
- a Honduran villager after the floods of 1998
- the Niagara Falls

Assessing your own progress

Generally, active learning is more effective than passive learning. You need to get as actively involved in your studies as possible. The skills listed above will help you to do this. By using your senses, your memory and your imagination, you will study much more efficiently than if you just sit back and hope that it will somehow happen. You need to be the driver, alert, aware of where you are going - not a passenger dozing off in the back seat.

One way of getting involved is to monitor your own progress regularly. This will help you identify any weaknesses when the time for revision comes along. All good home study courses include regular self-testing activities which will help you to achieve this goal.

ACTIVITY 24

Note: if you are studying more than one subject, you should do this activity once for each subject, making separate lists of relevant skills.

1. Look carefully at the study skills discussed in Sections B and C of this chapter.
2. Think of how necessary or unnecessary each skill is for the subject you are studying.
3. Allocate a number from 1 to 5 according to how important you think the skill is for your subject.
4. Give the skill '1' if you think it is absolutely necessary.
5. Give it '5' if you think it is totally irrelevant.
6. Now give a letter from A to E according to how competent you think you are at each skill.
7. Give the skill 'A' if you are completely competent.
8. Give the skill 'E' if you are no good at it at all.
9. Now look at the marks you have given to each skill.

A's and B's and 1's and 2's are fine. A score of B1 or A2 suggests that you know how to use the skills you know are important in your subject.

If you have scored D4 or E5 for a particular skill, you may not need this skill in your subject of study. (Ask your tutor to confirm this.)

Scores of D2, E1 etc., however, suggest that you need to practise this skill carefully, since it *is* necessary for your course, but you are not yet very good at it.

If possible, discuss your responses to this activity with your tutor.

D STUDY DIFFICULTIES AND HOW TO OVERCOME THEM

This whole book is designed to help you identify study difficulties and then overcome them. The other three sections in this chapter deal with specific study skills. This section takes a number of typical problems and refers these to the relevant chapters and sections of the book. It functions rather like a problem-solving index. Sarah, Ibrahim, Phillipa, Shefali and Alan tell us about the problems they have faced while studying, and how they went about finding solutions.

Phillipa says: 'My Psychology course began well. I was really enjoying it. But after three months the lease on my flat expired and I had to move out. I couldn't find a big enough place. I had nowhere to put all my books and papers. In my old flat I could spread things out and I knew where to find my work when I needed it. But in the new place everything is cramped and disorganised.

'So I got out my *How to Study* guide. I hadn't looked at it for ages. In Chapter 1, Section C, I found some helpful advice. Ideally, everything you need for studying should be arranged on shelves, or in a filing cabinet. But if you don't have enough space, you can store your stuff in cardboard boxes. The important thing is to label everything and keep it in some kind of order.

'So I went to the supermarket and got four big boxes. My notes were already arranged by topic. I put these into two of the boxes and wrote the topics on the front with a thick black pen. My study pack and my textbook went into the third box, together with pens, pencils and blank paper. And I put my reference books (an English dictionary, a dictionary of Psychology, and a thesaurus) into the last box. Finally, I stacked the boxes in the corner of my room, so that they were out of the way when I wasn't using them.'

Ibrahim says: 'Right from the start I had problems with my GCSE French. I really wanted that job in Africa, but the work seemed too hard. I didn't have a picture of what I had to do or where I was going.

'So I telephoned my student adviser and asked her what I should do. She asked whether I had the syllabus and past exam papers. I'd forgotten to send off for these. She also suggested I took a closer look at the *How to Study* book.

'I hadn't bothered with the Study Guide much when it arrived in the post. I was too keen to get on with the French course. Anyway I thought I knew how to study. But now I realised that I should have done some background work first. So I wrote to the examining board and got the syllabus and exam papers. Now I had a clearer picture of the whole course and what I was meant to do.

'Then I received a reminder in the post from Oxford Open Learning, telling me I ought to look for an exam centre without delay. It was a good thing I didn't leave it any longer, because it took several visits to exam centres before I found one that was willing to allow me to sit. If I'd waited much longer, I would have missed my chance, and what a waste that would have been!'

Alan says:'At first I was really keen to study. I want to get promotion, and I'm tired of the other guys in my platoon pulling my leg because I haven't got any qualifications. They say I'm thick!

'For the first six weeks I studied every day. I was making good progress. But studying is tough! The guys would interrupt me when I was just opening up my study pack and I'd get dragged off to play pool. So I skipped a day, then two days, then a whole week. I began to feel useless. All my dreams were slipping away from me.

'I phoned Lloyd, my Maths tutor, to ask his advice. What should I do? He said I needed to re-start my Study Plan. 'Don't be too ambitious,' he said. 'Spend half an hour a

day for a week, until you're back on track. Then build up from there. Look at your *How to Study* guide for other ideas.'

'So I tried it, and it worked. I had a talk with my mates and they agreed to leave me alone at set times. I also looked up Section C of Chapter 2 in the *How to Study* guide, where I found some advice about time management. I also read up on motivation in Section A of Chapter 2, and on developing my self-image in Section A of Chapter 1. Finally, I found advice about how to deal with interruptions in Section C of Chapter 4.

'After a couple of weeks I was doing two hours' studying each day. I photocopied my study timetable and gave a copy to each of my friends. That made it official. They realised I was serious and stopped pestering me when I was busy.'

Sarah says:'I found the GCSE Business Studies course very exciting, but the Accounting was gobbledygook to me. There was too much new material. I got so worried about this that I couldn't sleep. I persuaded my doctor to give me some sleeping pills but they just made me feel stupid. I couldn't do anything. I certainly couldn't study.

'So I stopped taking them. Then I read Chapter 6 of the *How to Study* guide. I started going for a mile-long walk each day to get some fresh air and exercise. I felt a bit more positive and decided it was time to get organised. So, as it advises in Chapter 2, Section C, I looked at the syllabus and some past papers and tried to work out what I already knew. My tutor told me this is called 'prior knowledge'.

'By referring back to the topics listed in the syllabus I could identify the parts I already knew something about. I looked up the *How to Study* guide again and re-did Activity 7 from Section C of Chapter 2. This boosted my self-confidence, because I realised I already knew something about some of the main topics, such as accounting data and verification of accounting records.

'I identified my problem areas as limited liability companies, manufacturing concerns, and the analyisis of accounting systems. At least I now knew where to concentrate my energies!'

Shefali says: 'I worked consistently until about three months before the exam. I was fascinated by Biology. The *How to Study* guide helped with its practical advice and related activities.

'I knew I was doing well. The feedback from my tutor was very positive. I telephoned her at least once a month, and when I had a problem she sorted it out for me quickly. My marks on the TMAs ranged from just about OK to very good. I got 90% for one assignment. I was proud of that.

'But around the middle of March things started to go wrong. I found it more and more difficult to concentrate on my studies. I started inventing all kinds of reasons to do something else — anything but study. Only a week earlier my desk was where I belonged, but suddenly I just couldn't sit there any more.

'It took me a few days to identify the problem. The closer the exams, the more worried I became. I was terrified of failing! I called up both my tutor and my student adviser and they basically told me the same thing: "You're doing fine. Don't panic. Carry on studying. Don't worry about the exam. Get some practice at exam technique, particularly working against the clock, and everything will be alright."

'My tutor also referred me to the *How to Study* guide, which I hadn't paid much attention to. After all, I thought I already knew everything about how to study!

'I looked up Chapter 7 (the one about exam preparation) and worked through some of the activities. This made me less panicky. I also read the first section of Chapter 5: this helped too. By getting regular practice at how to approach the exam, I managed to reduce my fear to a minimum. I still had butterflies in my stomach, but the whole experience was nothing like as bad as I had anticipated. And, yes, I passed in the end!'

ACTIVITY 25

1. Read about the study problems faced by the following students (Mike, Doreen, Gwen, Ali and Lionel.)

2. Imagine you are the students' tutors.

3. Look up and note down which sections of the *How to Study* guide each of them should work through in order to help them with their problems.

4. Write brief notes on the advice you would give each student over the telephone.

Mike says: 'I didn't have too many difficulties with the course itself, but I'm running into trouble now it's time for revision. I feel like my head is full of stuff and I can't see the wood for the trees. What should I do?'

Doreen says: 'I like the course I'm doing, which is 'A' level Government and Politics. But I'm having trouble getting the assignments in on time. I'm falling behind and my tutor has to keep phoning me to ask what's happening. I suppose I'm a perfectionist. I always think there's room for improvement. I can't let go. My assignments never seem to be finished. What can I do about this?'

Gwen says: 'I'm doing GCSE Geography. I can't read maps properly. I always get the wrong co-ordinates. Maybe that's because I don't have any sense of direction. Also, I don't understand the assignment questions. I read all the material in the modules, but when it comes to activities and assignments, I don't know what to do. How can I solve these problems?'

Steve says: 'I seem to spend all my time getting organised, but I never get started on the actual work. Yesterday I spent an hour tidying my desk, sharpening my pencils and filing my notes on GCSE Sociology. By the time I'd finished doing that there was no time left for studying, so I went to the pub and had a couple of pints to try to forget all about it. What can I do?'

Lionel says: 'I'm really determined to succeed. I'm doing GCSE Chemistry and Physics. I'm studying for five hours every day, on top of doing a full-time job. I really haven't got time to go out and see people, and I won't let my friends in when I'm busy. I even cancelled my subscription at the local gym so I could concentrate on my studies.

'Although I'm working really hard, I'm not feeling too good. I'm tired all the time and I'm finding it hard to concentrate. My skin is getting spotty and my girlfriend says I'm becoming very irritable.'

4 INTERACTING WITH YOUR TUTOR, OXFORD OPEN LEARNING, AND OTHERS

A YOU AND YOUR TUTOR

Your tutor is a valuable resource

This section explains how and when you should communicate with your tutor. All Oxford Open Learning students should read this section. There is an additional section below, Section AA. Only those students who are enrolled at their local college need to read Section AA.

Your tutor is your most valuable resource. Every tutor has been selected by Oxford Open Learning as an expert in his or her field. Oxford Open Learning's tutors are experienced teachers and lecturers who are thoroughly familiar with the syllabuses and course content of their subjects. They also know how your work will be assessed, including any course or project work, and how your exams are structured.

Don't be afraid to telephone your tutor! As an enrolled student, you have the right to do so. If you encounter a problem in your studies, read to the end of the lesson you are working on. If the problem remains, write down exactly what the difficulty is, together with details of the module, lesson and page number, and contact your tutor at once. It is a mistake to wait until later: telephone your tutor while the difficulty is still fresh in your mind.

Remember: your tutor is your helper. Tutors are paid to answer your calls. Your tutor will be delighted to hear from you!

Use your lessons

There's no point in contacting your tutor until you have something to discuss. So before we examine your relationship with your tutor, let's look again at how you can improve your study performance while working alone.

When working through the study pack, most students prefer not to read the lessons straight through from beginning to end. It is far more effective to read just two or three paragraphs at a time. Then you should stop and *think* and see if you can recall the main points.

Next, read the same short section again. You may find that you now understand some aspects of the lesson more clearly than you did on your first reading.

This technique involves dividing your studies up into short, manageable segments. It also allows you to become more actively involved in your work.

As you read through each lesson, underline or highlight the key points. This concentrates your understanding. It also helps you to make accurate notes, and is invaluable when you re-read your lessons later during revision. There are wide margins to the left of the text in each lesson. These are designed to give you enough space to add your own notes or ideas.

Make notes

You will find it helpful to make notes as you study: keep a notebook, preferably with large pages, for this purpose. At the end of each section, go back over what you have read and write down the main points. This is where the idea of highlighting will prove useful. Making notes will strongly reinforce your learning at the time. Your notebook will also be invaluable when you embark on your revision programme (see Chapter 6, Section A).

Test yourself

Before attempting a Self-Assessment Test (SAT) or Practice Test at the end of a lesson, read through your notes and check the points you have highlighted. If you cannot remember some of the details, quickly read through the relevant section again. Then do the SAT.

When you have completed the SAT, compare your answers with the model answers, which appear either at the back of the module or at the end of the course. Again, if you have given incorrect answers, take another look at your notes and your highlighted points. If necessary, read through the relevant lesson one more time, making sure that you have not missed any of the main points. If you are still unable to understand the correct answers, make a note of the exact module, lesson and page reference, and telephone your tutor without delay!

ACTIVITY 1

1. Choose the next lesson of new material from your study pack that ends with a Self-Assessment Test (SAT).
2. Read through the lesson, highlighting the main points.
3. Stop every two or three paragraphs to make sure that you have understood what you are reading.
4. If necessary, go back and read the paragraphs again.

5. When you reach the end of the lesson, look over the highlighted points once more.
6. Use your highlighted points to make notes in your notebook. Practise the abbreviation and note-making techniques described in Section 3 of Chapter 3.
7. Set aside your notes and attempt the SAT.
8. Check your answers against the suggested answers given in your study pack.
9. If your answers are incorrect, go back to your notes and to the lesson itself.
10. Read the material again, trying to identify where you have made mistakes.

Submitting assignments

It is most important that all Tutor-Marked Assignments (TMAs) are completed and sent for assessment, because:

- they consolidate your learning;
- they show your tutor how you are progressing;
- they enable your tutor to help you with any difficulties;
- they give you invaluable examination experience.

By all means revise before attempting an assignment. However, once you have started the assignment, keep your study material and notes out of sight. Any points that you have not fully grasped will then show up in your answers. That is precisely what you want to happen, so that your tutor can help you.

Your tutor will assess your work, comment on it and give you a mark. You will also be sent a set of Suggested Answers. Great care is always taken in assessing the hard work you have put into your assignments, and this naturally takes time. You should allow around 10 days before you expect your marked assignments to be returned to you, and longer during holiday periods. On occasion, there may also be postal delays.

Do remember that your tutors are not there to catch you out. *They are there to help you*, and it is your written responses that enable them to do just that.

Presentation of assignments

The following guidelines will help you to ensure that your assignments are clear and readable, that they receive the full attention of your tutor, and that they are returned to you speedily.

- When you receive this *How to Study* guide, you should also receive an envelope containing various useful documents, including a set of Tutor-Marked Assignment Cover Sheets, one of which should be completed and sent with each assignment.
- Use A4 or foolscap size paper.
- Leave a good left-hand margin, where your tutor can write comments.
- Do not pad out your answers with unnecessary words; make your assignments as concise and accurate as possible.
- Write neatly, leaving plenty of space. Divide your work into paragraphs, which should not be too long. Either leave a blank line between paragraphs or indent the first line of each paragraph. If you type your answers, use double spacing.
- Attempt to answer every question (unless instructed otherwise).
- Don't send more than one assignment at a time. This will allow you to rectify any weaknesses that are pointed out by your tutor, before proceeding further.
- Where possible, attach the TMA Cover Sheet itself to your answer sheets.
- Send all the answers for a particular assignment in one envelope.

- For extra security, keep a photocopy of the assignment. Then if the original gets lost, you won't have to rewrite it!

The TMA Cover Sheets

Make sure you attach a TMA Cover Sheet to each assignment that you send in. You will find a set of cover sheets in the document envelope that accompanies this *How to Study* guide.

The student completes the top half of the Cover Sheet before sending the work to the tutor. The tutor will complete the bottom half. The Cover Sheet will still be attached to the assignment when it comes back to you.

Please note that the final section, 'Date Leaving Tutor', may indicate a date some time before the assignment reaches you. This is because the tutor will normally send the assignment back via Oxford Open Learning.

Here, the marks will be recorded, and sets of Suggested Answers and possibly other documents, will be added. All this takes time, so please be patient. Normally, a short delay should not cause you any problems, as you will carry on with the next phase of your studies meanwhile.

Marks awarded

As well as making constructive comments, your tutor should give you a mark for each assignment. This will be a percentage or a mark out of a given total, such as 13/20. In some courses, the tests have their own mark schemes, usually based on the mark scheme used in the examination.

If you have not mastered a topic and as a result you receive a low mark, your tutor will show where your difficulty lies. You should revise the relevant lesson attempt the assignment again and compare your answers with the specimen answers provided.

Do *not* resubmit an assignment unless specifically requested to do so by your tutor. If you have scored less than 30%, you may well be asked to resubmit. Don't take this personally – everyone has the occasional off day.

Don't panic if you get low marks at the beginning of your course. Some courses start with quite a difficult test, while others ease you in more gradually. Never use a disappointing mark as an excuse for abandoning your Study Plan or missing even a single session of study.

A low mark may simply be a sign that you have not started the course with as much background knowledge as some other students. This may well be so if you are attempting an 'A' level without having passed a GCSE in the same subject. But if you are patient and keep to your Study Plan, you will gradually catch up with the students who already have that knowledge.

It may help you to keep a record of the date on which you send each assignment for assessment and the date on which it is returned. The *Assignment Date Record Form* has been designed to help you keep track of your assignments. You will find a copy of this form in the document envelope that was sent to you with this *How to Study* guide.

Telephone contact: ringing your tutor

The most successful open learning students are generally those who make best use of the telephone. If they don't understand something, they call their tutor, who is usually able to solve the problem.

Your tutor is paid to answer your calls, so don't hesitate to take advantage of this service, however small your difficulty. Ringing your tutor shows that you can identify your problems, that you care about your studies, and that you have the initiative to ask for help. As far as your tutor is concerned, your call is a good sign, not a bad one.

Sometimes you will not be able to get through to your tutor directly. Leave a message, saying what your problem is, and when you will be available. Your tutor will normally call back within 24 hours. Try to make sure you are in when you've said you'll be in to receive the tutor's call.

Tutors can help you best if you tell them exactly what the problem is. If you just say 'I don't understand algebra' or '*The Mill on the Floss* doesn't make any sense to me', you are not giving your tutor much chance of helping you effectively. The problem is too vague and wide-ranging to be solved over the phone.

It is much better if you can identify specific small-scale problems which can be tackled one at a time (see *Breaking up large tasks into smaller units* in Chapter 3, Section C).

If you say 'the word "protectionism" is used on p. 7 of Lesson 12, but I've no idea what it means', your tutor has a good chance of helping you, because your question is clear, focused and precise. If your problem relates to a particular part of the course, quote the module, lesson and page number. If it relates to an accompanying textbook, give all the details, but remember that tutors cannot be expected to know all supporting textbooks from cover to cover.

Tutors are only human and it is easy to make mistakes over the phone. The time of your call may be inconvenient or the tutor may not be able to give you an answer immediately.

There are other reasons why you might telephone your tutor. You may want to change your Study Plan, or to discuss your coursework or exams.

Taking calls from your tutor

Your tutor may ring you, perhaps to discuss your last assignment or because you haven't sent in any work for some time. He or she is not there to give you problems, but rather to offer you friendly advice and encouragement. Remember that your tutor is on your side - the tutor wants you to succeed almost as much as you do.

The Oxford Open Learning system achieves much of its success because tutors are obliged to keep in touch with you on a regular basis, usually by phone. So they will want to know when they can ring you and expect to be able to speak to you. Please be as cooperative as you can and make sure that you really are there when you have said you will be, to pick up the receiver and talk sensibly about your study progress.

If you have good reason to think that your tutor will be calling at a certain time and you know you won't be available after all, it is courteous to phone your tutor beforehand to explain and to save your tutor the trouble of needlessly calling you. And if your tutor has left a message for you, ring back as soon as possible.

There may come a time when you have not managed to get an assignment in by the agreed date and, as a result, you are dreading the tutor's call. Whatever you do, do *not* persuade someone else to take the tutor's call and say you are out. It's a short cut from there to losing the thread of your studies altogether.

Take that call. Your tutor will not be angry that your work has not appeared. The tutor genuinely wants you to succeed and is worried about the missed assignment. For that reason he or she will ask you to settle on a new date for submitting the work. You may also have to consider whether you can still keep to your original Study Plan, or whether you need to devise a new one.

Whether or not you are making good progress, your tutor really will appreciate it if you are ready to take that call. You also need to have a clear sense of how the tutor can help you. It's your big chance, after all! You're not paying for the call, and you have the undivided, individual attention of your teacher. Make the most of it. Home learners spend much less contact time with their teacher than students in a classroom and it is vital to get the most out of these precious moments.

Is there anything you shouldn't ask?

The general rule of thumb is that you can ask your tutor anything that relates directly to your study pack or to the syllabus. But you cannot expect your tutor to give you advice beyond that.

Let's say you are studying Information Technology, for instance. This does not mean that you are entitled to ring up your tutor every time your computer crashes or you have trouble loading software (especially if it is illegal!). Don't put your tutor in the embarrassing position of having to say no.

Nor are tutors professional careers advisers, so don't expect your tutor to offer you help with your long-term plans.

Problems with coursework

Consult your tutor about the content of your coursework projects *before* you begin work on them. Ensure that your proposed topic or subject area meets the exam board's requirements.

Your tutor is available to advise you about your coursework, but not to do the work for you! Your tutor is going to have to sign a form to say that all the coursework you have done is your own unaided work, so do not try to push your tutor into giving you more help than the exam board allows. It is also up to you to get your coursework folder organised. It's no good blaming your tutor if you don't!

Make a photocopy of your coursework and keep this safely in case the original gets lost. Always send your coursework by recorded delivery. Remember that it is *your* responsibility to know what the exam board requires (and when!). Make sure you submit your coursework, and the necessary paperwork, in good time.

Personal problems

There is often a thin dividing line between personal problems and study problems, because personal problems can affect your ability to study. By all means make your tutor aware, in general terms, of the problem that is affecting your studies. But do not treat your tutor as a psychiatrist or as a shoulder to cry on.

Develop a professional relationship with your tutor, and out of professional respect may come an element of friendship, but don't expect any more than that.

A working relationship

If you are linked to a local college, there may be some opportunity to meet your tutor, but that won't be true for most readers of this book. You may find you are within travelling range of your tutor, but in all probability meetings will still be out of the question.

Some students (especially those who are making little or no progress) form the opinion that their tutor is ringing too often. This is an odd view. Your tutor is paid to help you, and this is all he or she is trying to do. Even if your tutor rings at an inconvenient time, you should always be polite and helpful. This will mean that you will receive more of your tutor's time and attention when you really do need help.

Cherish your tutor. As a home learner, a good working relationship with your tutor is one of your most important assets. It's up to you to get the most out of it.

Written enquiries

If you don't mind waiting a few days for a reply, it is often better to write to your tutor rather than telephone. This is especially true if your problem is a long or complex one. A written enquiry gives your tutor time to think through the problem and to work out the best possible answer. Usually, your tutor will phone you back with the answer, so when you write, try to suggest a suitable time when you can be contacted. For example, if you post your enquiry first class on a Monday, you could suggest times for the tutor to phone you on Tuesday or Wednesday.

A suitable form, headed *Enquiry Note*, is also provided in the document envelope which accompanies this *How to Study* guide. You can use this form to state your problem or as a cover sheet for a longer written enquiry to your tutor. If necessary, you can make as many copies of the form as you like.

Holidays

You may or may not go away on holiday during your period of study – that's up to you. If you do so, it's courteous to let your tutor know.

Tutors are also entitled to go on holiday from time to time, and they are asked to let people know well in advance if they will be away for more than a week.

If your tutor goes away, it will normally be between mid-June and the end of August. This is when the fewest assignments come in. If possible, plan your assignment diary to take account of your tutor's annual holiday. Please be patient at this time.

There is one time of year, however, when you can expect your tutor to take about 10 days' break without giving you notice. This is over Christmas and the New Year. So at this time, be prepared to wait a while for the return of your assignments. And unless it's an emergency, try to avoid telephoning your tutor between about 20 December and 2 January.

Thinking of suspending your studies?

You may have to stop studying temporarily for a specific reason. For instance, a baby is expected, a relative dies, or you are moving house. One of the advantages of home study is that this is not necessarily a long-term problem. You don't have to give up altogether. Instead, you can reduce your study time or suspend your studies for a few weeks, or even longer, until you can return to your normal study routine.

If you are thinking of suspending your course, for whatever reason, please let your tutor know. As soon as you are ready, start studying again and send in another assignment. You can leave a gap between assignments of up to a year and you can take your exam up to three years after enrolment, syllabus permitting.

Don't interrupt your Study Plan for too long!

A word of warning, however. Experience suggests that there are dangers attached to suspending your studies. Most students genuinely believe that they can stop studying for a few weeks and then pick up from where they left off. But in many cases time goes by, and the student never returns to his or her books. Of students who suspend their studies for a month or more, only 10% ever resume studying and pass the exam. Don't assume that you are any different!

How can you avoid the possibility that you will never return to your studies? Instead of suspending your studies altogether, *reduce* the number of study sessions. But make sure that your reduced Study Plan is clear to both you and your tutor, and then stick to it!

You also need to be clear how long you are going to work to your reduced Study Plan. Identify a specific date when you will return to your normal Study Plan, and make sure you do so.

Continuity is crucial. Very few students have the ability to manage a stop-start approach successfully, so don't risk it. Think of all the work that will be wasted if you get out of the habit of studying. Remind yourself *why* you are studying, and recommit yourself to those goals.

The summer is the worst time. July and August should be written in red for danger on your personal calendar. More students fall by the wayside during the summer months than at any other time of year. The weather's fine, the days are long, outdoor sports beckon, and others are having fun. Nobody else is studying: they all finished their exams in June. Perhaps you're off on holiday yourself for a couple of weeks.

It's a big problem – no doubt about it. But as long as you remember how important it is not to get out of the habit of studying, you should be able to cope. Revise your Study Plan, perhaps, but when you've done that, stick to it. If you can't bear to take your textbooks away with you on holiday, try to think of the most enjoyable aspect of your course and spend a bit of time on that while you are away. Ask your friends and family to give you the right sort of encouragement through this difficult time.

And if you make it through to September and your studies are still very much on track, give yourself a big pat on the back. You deserve it!

Thinking of giving up altogether?

Very occasionally, a student has to give up studying. We sincerely hope that this does not happen to you.

If you are tempted to give up, think carefully about it and talk it over with your tutor. Your tutor will give an honest opinion of your progress so far and your prospects for the examination. Sometimes you may already have done enough work to have a good chance of passing the examination.

If you think of giving up, bear in mind all the hard work that will go to waste. If you stop studying, even for a few months, you are likely to forget a lot of what you have learnt, so you owe it to yourself to continue.

Some students find one topic difficult or dull, some another. There is a good chance that the next topic will be easier or more interesting. If at all possible, continue with your course. Then, after a few months, you will have finished the course and passed the examination.

AA YOU, YOUR TUTOR, AND YOUR TUTOR'S COLLEGE (for college-linked students only)

You and your tutor

Your tutor is crucial to your chances of success. Get to know your tutor and make the most of their services. Your tutor is an experienced professional, trained to get results, but your tutor can only help you if you allow this to happen.

You are lucky that you have been fixed up with a tutor who lives fairly locally. Your tutor may be in the same city or the same county and is probably within range of a local call. This has the effect of making telephone calls much cheaper, so do ring up when you need help.

Very few tutors spend their whole day marking assignments. Most are full-time adult educators who keep closely in touch with the latest curriculum developments.

As professionals, they are generally under contract to their main employer, the local college of further education (CFE). For your tutor to teach you, you are required to enrol at the college. You may already have been asked to fill in a college enrolment form.

This is just a formality but it must be done straight away. It does not commit you to anything. You will not have to go into college for lessons (unless the syllabus includes practical requirements). You will not have to meet your tutor if you don't want to. You might not set foot in the college until you take your examinations. It does not even matter if you move away from the area (you can keep the same tutor).

The information you give on the enrolment form will not be passed on to anyone - it remains absolutely confidential - so please fill in the forms as soon as you receive them.

The benefits of enrolment

The fact that your tutor is employed and you are enrolled at the same college is of great benefit to you. The advantages are that:

- you can ask your tutor for roughly five hours of personal face-to-face tuition each year, at no extra cost (details may vary slightly from college to college);
- you may use that personal tuition to sort out coursework or practical requirements (if these are part of the syllabus);
- your tutor may be in a position to mark your coursework (this is not possible for most home learners whose tutor is not local);

- you may take books out of the college library, eat in the canteen, and use other college facilities such as the bookshop and career guidance services, if you want to;
- you may take the examination at the college, which means that all the exam administration is taken care of.

Some colleges offer additional benefits. It is up to you whether you make use of these opportunities or not.

One other advantage of enrolling at a college is that it has made your course cheaper. The college gets funding from the government and a small part of that comes to Oxford Open Learning. We would not be able to offer the course materials, tuition and administrative support, etc., for such a low price if it were not for this funding.

How you make use of the college is entirely up to you. Having enrolled, you can ignore the college altogether if you prefer. But our advice is to make the most of all this free support. Making progress on your own is not easy. The more people you can get to help you the better. The only thing they can't do for you is the studying itself!

Face-to-face tutorials

If you are linked to a local college in this way, you will probably be offered the chance to arrange some personal tutorials when you need them. For some students, this can make all the difference between success and failure. However good a student you are, there are bound to be aspects of the course that you find difficult. A phone call may help, but sometimes a more detailed discussion is useful and it may be worth asking for a tutorial.

Who arranges the tutorial? Usually the student, but in certain subjects, a good tutor will set up tutorials for you. In practical subjects, like Chemistry, where laboratory work is involved, the tutor will probably arrange group sessions, usually outside normal working hours.

But in other subjects, it is generally up to the student to ask for a tutorial. It is not necessary to have a particular topic that you want to discuss, although it will certainly help if you can tell your tutor exactly where you have got to in your studies. You should also identify any difficulties you are having with the course.

Sometimes a tutor will notice that you have had problems with an assignment and will suggest that you come in for a tutorial session. If this happens, it's best to take the tutor's advice.

The tutorial will take place either at the tutor's home or at the college where the tutor works. The timing of the tutorial is a matter for discussion between tutor and student. Most tutors are very flexible regarding their working hours but there may be limitations on the use of college facilities. Your tutor will always try to fit in with your personal preferences.

How many tutorials can you have? This varies from college to college but the general rule is a maximum of five hours of individual face-to-face tuition per academic year. If tutorials are arranged in pairs, the maximum is ten hours. If you take tutorials in groups of four, you may receive up to 20 hours of teaching time, and so on.

If you want more than the agreed amount of face-to-face tuition, you will have to pay for it. Your tutor or college will let you know how to proceed.

What happens if you have to miss a tutorial? This is not a big problem as long as you give your tutor plenty of warning. Don't wait until just before the agreed time and then try to cancel your tuition.

Worst of all, don't just 'forget' to turn up. This is very unfair to your tutor, who has made special arrangements to teach you. It will certainly count as one of your allotted hours. If it happens more than once, you will not be offered any further tutorial time.

So make the most of this opportunity. When you meet your tutor face to face, it gives you the chance to build a good working relationship. It is therefore a good idea to schedule the first tutorial soon after you start the course. Don't be shy. It will give you a big advantage in the long run.

Are tutorials ever compulsory? Only if you are doing a science subject such as Physics, Chemistry or Biology where the syllabus requires laboratory work. In all other subjects you have the option of working entirely from home.

Please note that the system varies from college to college. Some colleges are more flexible and helpful than others. Please co-operate with the system that is offered to you, remembering that Oxford Open Learning has to turn many students away because we can't find a local tutor for them. You are fortunate to live in a place where a local tutor is available.

Contacting your tutor's college

With most problems, you should first call your tutor, but sometimes it will be necessary to contact your college's central office. Here are some reasons why:

1. to arrange examination entry;
2. to discuss financial questions, such as the cost of additional personal tuition;

3. to discuss administrative problems; for example, if an assignment has gone astray or if some of your course materials are missing;
4. to make enquiries about taking further courses of study;
5. to record changes of personal details; for example, if you have changed address.

B YOU AND OXFORD OPEN LEARNING

Contacting Oxford Open Learning

Your tutor is normally the person to contact regarding any aspect of your course. Sometimes, however, you may need to contact your student adviser or another official at Oxford Open Learning's central office. Here are some possible reasons:

1. to discuss financial problems: if you are having trouble paying your instalments in time or if you are experiencing any other financial difficulty;
2. to discuss administrative problems: for example, if an assignment has gone astray or if some of your course materials are missing;
3. to make enquiries about taking further courses of study;
4. to notify Oxford Open Learning of changes of personal details such as a change of address;
5. to give details of other potential customers for courses of study - please ask their permission first! (If any of these people do become students in the following three months, you are entitled to claim £10 commission);
6. (this applies to locally-enrolled students only) if you experience any problems in the relationship between you and your tutor's college which the college is unable to sort out.

You can contact Oxford Open Learning by telephone on 0870 789 0800 or by writing to:

Oxford Open Learning
FREEPOST OF2309
Oxford
OX2 0YZ

C YOU AND OTHER PEOPLE

This section offers some advice about how to prevent disruptive people from interfering with your studies. It also suggests ways of making use of other people who may be able to help. Before reading through this section, you could re-read the parts of Chapter 1, Section C that deal with other people.

People who disrupt your studies

These may be your friends or colleagues, or members of your family. Tell all the people who are likely to disturb you, either by telephone or in person, of your Study Plan and your weekly timetable. If possible, write out your timetable and display it in a suitable place so that everyone you live with knows when you will be busy. You can also photocopy your timetable and give it to your friends.

Don't attempt to study all day every day. It's unhealthy, and your family and friends will wonder where you have gone. Build into your Study Plan times when you *can*

socialise, when you *will* be available to spend time with other people.

If your home environment is too crowded, or too noisy, for you to be able to study in peace, or if the people you live with refuse to understand your need for quiet, think about studying somewhere else. The obvious place is the local library. Nowadays many public libraries are equipped with study booths expressly designed for this purpose.

If you are working, you may be able to find a corner of an office where you can study, perhaps during your lunch hour, or before or after your hours of work. Or you may know someone who will let you use their work space for a few hours a week. Call your tutor if you are experiencing real difficulty finding a suitable study environment.

People who may be able to help with your studies

There are advantages in studying from home. You are your own boss, so nobody can tell you what to do. Also, the time scale of your studies is much more flexible than if you attend college.

But studying on your own requires determination and a sense of responsibility. Because you are your own boss, you have to make all the decisions. You have to be in control. Sometimes it can be a lonely business.

That's why it's useful to get the assistance of anyone who can provide support or advice in your studies. If you know an expert in your subject, contact them. But helpers need not be familiar with the subject in order to play a positive role.

The most important qualities your helper needs are willingness, sympathy and patience. You need to explain clearly what you are studying and why (see Section A of Chapter 2) so that your helper knows the purpose behind your efforts.

Remember that *you* are in charge of your studies. It is up to you to plan your work so that you can make the best and most economical use of your helper's time.

Here are some ways in which another person can help you with your studies:

- by reading through a lesson that you find difficult and then discussing it with you;
- by making notes on the key points of a particular topic and then comparing their version with yours;

- by encouraging you without being judgmental;
- by listening to your problems and offering advice;
- by testing you on particular topics according to your requirements (this is especially useful during revision);
- by allowing you to teach them; in other words, you explain a topic you have studied: if the other person understands it, you can be fairly sure that you have understood it yourself!

Other students

If you are able to make contact with one or more people who are currently studying the same course as you, or who have studied the same course recently, it's a good idea to do so. The opportunity to meet and share ideas can be extremely rewarding. Here are some suggestions for working together:

- Develop cooperation and teamwork, rather than competitiveness. This doesn't mean that you should work together on assignments, but rather than you should share responsibilities and ideas.
- Try to provide mutual support. Invite one another to identify topics or tasks that are particularly difficult. Pool your resources in solving such problems.
- Meet regularly if possible. A weekly two-hour meeting would be appropriate, but this depends on the needs and commitments of the individuals.
- Whenever you meet, finish off by planning the next meeting. Agree that each member of the group (even if there are only two of you) should carry out

a particular task before the next meeting and report back to the group on what they have achieved. This might involve, for example, researching a particular topic and giving a five-minute presentation.

Computer contact

Oxford Open Learning runs an automated mailing list for each course title. Oxford Open Learning students are all invited to subscribe to the mailing list for the subject(s) they are studying. Students who are enrolled at their local college may complete a special form, giving their e-mail address to Oxford Open Learning, and they too will be included on the list.

Every e-mail message sent to the list is copied to all subscribers. So, for instance, a Geography GCSE student may send his or her message to geography@ool.co.uk and all the other students on the Geography GCSE list, as well as the Geography tutors, will receive the message and have the opportunity to reply in the same way.

D OXFORD OPEN LEARNING'S PROMISE

Your money back if you fail

No one wants to fail. There is no reason why you should fail. But to soften the blow if you do fail, Oxford Open Learning offers to return *all your fees*. All you have to do is to send proof of failure (e.g. the exam certificate) and the money will be sent straight back to you.

Please note the following conditions to our money-back guarantee:

1. the student must have completed all assignments in the course, earning a mark of at least 30% in each assignment;
2. a pass at 'A' level is considered to be any grade between A and E; at GCSE, it is any grade between A* and E;
3. the student must provide written proof of exam failure to qualify for a refund;
4. the student must have paid all the required fees on time; if paying by instalment, the student should have been no more than 3 weeks late with any payment.

No refund is available unless all these conditions are met. In particular, it means that you must have attempted every assignment. This is for your own good - the course has been written in such a way that the successful student does no more and no less than the complete set of assignments. This amounts to less work than you would have to do if you were on a full-time course but it should be enough to allow you to aim for the top grades.

What if you fail the exam without having submitted all the assignments? No refund is available in these circumstances. However, you are entitled to continue studying and submitting assignments, with a view to taking the exam again the following year. And we would strongly encourage you to do so!

These are competitive exams and some students do fail. Oxford Open Learning cannot be liable, under any circumstances, for more than the sum of money you have paid out. Nor is there any guarantee that a specific grade will be achieved. Oxford Open Learning cannot be liable if you fail to find an exam centre, or if the nearest exam centre proves to be further away than you would like – these things are beyond the control of Oxford Open Learning. Sorry!

Please see the money-back guarantee as a symbol of Oxford Open Learning's determination that you will succeed. The very fact that you have been accepted onto the programme is a sign that Oxford Open Learning believes that you are capable of success.

5 DEALING WITH STRESS

A CALMING YOURSELF DOWN

Too much pressure!

As your course progresses, the pressure will mount. The more you study, the more there is to remember. Keeping to your Study Plan may involve sacrifices. Sometimes you may feel irritated or angry. The effort to meet assignment deadlines may cause you additional worry. And of course, when the exams loom closer, nearly everybody starts to get nervous.

Section B of this chapter describes ways of keeping your body in good condition. Remember that your ability to think, study and remember depends on the efficient running of your whole body, not just what's happening inside your head. Exercise maintains the supply of blood to the brain. A healthy, well-rested body is less likely to suffer undue stress than one that has been neglected.

But no matter how well we look after ourselves, we cannot entirely avoid stressful situations. When we become angry or afraid a hormone called adrenalin is produced in the adrenal glands (near the kidneys) and released into the bloodstream. Adrenalin is a powerful stimulant that results in the following bodily changes:

- increased blood pressure
- faster heartbeat

- heightened alertness
- increased muscular strength
- shallower, more rapid breathing
- dryness in the mouth.

The release of adrenalin is completely beyond our conscious control. In our ancestral past, adrenalin was intended to help us either fight our enemies or run away. Unfortunately, in the exam venue, neither of these responses is appropriate! All too often a nervous candidate will find his body flooded with adrenalin, and with no way of using up the excess energy, the result is blind panic!

This section therefore offers some ways of limiting worry and fear. These techniques will help you deal with any stressful situation, but I have in mind particularly all the stressful situations you may encounter that relate to studying, revision and exams.

Breathe easy

If you are worried, angry, or simply very tired, try a simple breathing activity, which slows down the heartbeat and enriches the supply of oxygen to the brain. You might find it worth doing for two or three minutes just before an exam.

ACTIVITY 1

This activity involves a breathing sequence that can be repeated as necessary. The four phases of the sequence should happen in the timed ratio of 2-8-4-1 seconds. The activity works best with eyes closed.

1. Breathe in deeply. Silently count '1, 2' as you do so.

2. Hold your breath as you silently count from 1 to 8. Don't 'lock' the muscles of your throat or chest. Hold your breath as gently as possible.
3. Release your breath slowly as you count from 1 to 4.
4. Count '1' while your lungs remain empty.
5. Repeat instructions 1-4.

When you have practised this activity a few times, try slowing your breathing down. Make each number you count correspond to two seconds. (That means holding your breath for 16 seconds!)

A safe place in the mind

We all need to escape from the turmoil of our lives from time to time. Often there isn't the physical space available to do this. But there is nothing to stop us escaping from the stresses of the present, temporarily at least, in our *imagination*. By visualising a calmer, more peaceful environment, we can learn to calm ourselves down.

This is really nothing more than a focused kind of daydreaming, but it requires a certain amount of practice.

ACTIVITY 2

1. Sit somewhere quiet where you won't be disturbed for ten minutes.
2. Close your eyes and do the breathing exercise in Activity 1 three or four times.
3. Imagine a beautiful place you know or have seen pictures of, or invent one of your own.
4. Think about what you can see, hear, feel, taste and touch in this beautiful place.
5. Explore this environment in your imagination for a few minutes.
6. When you have finished, slowly open your eyes.

Dream on

We all dream, every night of our lives. Only a small part of our time asleep is spent dreaming. Some people remember dreams, others don't. Often, when we are very stressed, our dreams become more vivid, and perhaps also more disturbing.

It's important to 'get in touch with your dreams', especially if they're bothering you. Try keeping a notebook, or *dream diary* by your bed. When you wake up, spend five minutes

writing down whatever you can remember of your dreams. After a few days you'll find that your dream-memories become clearer. Keep your dream diary safely hidden during the daytime!

Touch

A simple hug is a great way to provide reassurance and to restore confidence. Touching the people you know and love provides a signal of trust and gives both people comfort. (Don't try this with strangers: you might find yourself charged with harassment!) If there's anyone nearby you can hug without causing offence, go and hug them!

The sensation of touch can also help to relieve stress, even if it involves an object rather than a person. Some people (even adults!) have a favourite teddy bear or cushion, which they hold on tight to in times of distress.

All kinds of objects can provide us with reassurance. Although I gave up smoking several years ago, I have a rectangular brass cigarette lighter which I often carry around in my pocket. I no longer even bother to fill it with lighter fuel. But I like it because it has a sentimental value and it fits snugly into the palm of my hand. For other people, worry beads and sucking stones serve the same sort of purpose as my lighter.

ACTIVITY 3

1. Select a number of objects that are nearby. Choose things of different shape, weight, and made of different materials. Don't choose anything sharp, jagged or dangerous.
2. Handle each object in turn. Close your eyes in order to concentrate on the sensation of touch.

Taking control

Nobody has total control over their lives. Even the most powerful people are subject to forces that they cannot always manipulate to their own advantage. But some people almost seem to *want* to become victims. After a bit of bad luck, whether it's with their studies, their work, or their lover, some people just give up.

A sense of hopelessness leads to negative thoughts and statements. This soon becomes a vicious circle. Whatever may be wrong with your life, it becomes increasingly difficult to do anything about it.

But think about this for a minute. The past is done. Whatever went wrong, you can't go back and change it. The best you can do is learn from your experiences, however difficult or painful they were. Change is only possible in the present and the future.

True, you can't change everything, but there are significant details of your life that you *can* change. And there are all kinds of ways in which your thoughts and actions can make such changes happen.

We've talked a lot about how important it is to turn your studies and your revision from a *passive* attempt to absorb information, into an *active* engagement with your work. The same principle applies to every other aspect of your life. You *can* make the world a better place for you (without making it worse for other people).

Negative attitudes can be reversed. It's a question of practice. Take a series of small steps. If you're feeling really low, you need to rebuild your self-esteem gradually (see Section A of Chapter 1).

ACTIVITY 4

1. Make a list of things that you are unhappy about in your life. Concentrate on your studies, but if there are other things that are really bothering you, include these as well.

2. Write brief notes about what you can do to improve the situation.

3. Plan how to put your ideas into action over the next few days or weeks.

Some stress is natural, even useful

Sometimes we get so stressed that we need to relax completely. Other techniques for reducing stress are described in Section B of this chapter below. But under certain circumstances, some stress can be useful. If you went into your exam completely relaxed, without a care in the world, you might be too laid back to bother to answer the questions!

Too much stress amounts to 'rubble in the road', as one friend of mine used to say. It blocks up the nervous system and prevents efficient functioning But in an exam, no stress at all may be just as bad. It's a question of getting the right quantity of stress, which results in maximum alertness, without undue anxiety.

Do you remember Activity 2, in which you imagined a calm, peaceful, beautiful place, a refuge from the noise and trouble of daily life? We can use the same technique of *visualisation* to train ourselves to deal with stress. The best way of channelling stress is to focus it on a specific situation.

The more generalised your worries are, the more difficult it is to do anything practical about them. If you can turn your stress to something specific, it becomes more real and at the same time, easier to deal with. Section B of Chapter 7 below encourages you to get as much actual practice of exam conditions as possible. Here, we concentrate on *imagining* what the exam will be like.

ACTIVITY 5

1. Close your eyes and do Activity 1 above (the breathing exercise) three or four times.
2. Now imagine, in as much detail as possible, the following events.
3. It is the morning of your exam. You wake up, get dressed, and grab a bite to eat.
4. You put everything you need for the exam into your bag and set off for the exam venue.
5. On the journey, you begin to get more and more nervous.
6. You arrive at the venue with 10 minutes to spare.
7. You go into the venue and find your seat.
8. You take your pens, pencils, etc. out of your bag and arrange them in front of you.
9. The invigilator hands round the question papers.

You are told to begin!

B GETTING ENOUGH FOOD, EXERCISE AND SLEEP

You are what you eat

Some people neglect themselves when they study. They become so convinced of the importance of their studies that they don't have time to do anything else. Don't fall into this trap! You need to balance your studying with a number of activities, and one of these is making sure you get enough healthy food to eat.

Make sure you get a balanced diet. We will look at what most people mean by a balanced diet (how much of what kinds of food) in a moment. But we also need a balance in terms of *when* we eat. These days many people skip breakfast altogether. This is not a good idea. Even if you don't feel hungry, you should eat something soon after you wake up, and within a couple of hours at the latest.

Remember that food is the fuel that your body and brain need to burn. Without food, there is no energy! And when you get up in the morning, your body has already gone without nutrition for at least six hours, and maybe ten or twelve, or even longer.

If you wait until lunchtime before you eat again, your body may have gone without food for as much as 16 hours. If you really can't cope with breakfast at all, then have a nutritious snack (a sandwich, or a small tub of yoghurt, or a couple of bananas) by mid-morning.

Some people eat their main meal at lunchtime, others in the evening. Ideally, your meals should be spread out evenly through the day. Avoid eating a huge meal shortly before you go to bed. It's impossible for our bodies to digest food properly when we are lying down. And food provides a big input of energy: we need this during the day, not late at night!

It's also worth noting that if you are agitated, food can calm you down. (Don't gulp the food down quickly, though, or you will get indigestion.) Milk, for example, contains a morphine-like substance. And you may have noticed that after a substantial meal, we often feel relaxed, even a little sleepy. This is because our bodies release chemicals called endomorphins, which cause a feeling of wellbeing. Even a glass of water, sipped slowly, can calm you down.

Here are some guidelines about eating, taken from one of Oxford Open Learning's Biology study packs:

> *A balanced diet must include carbohydrates, fats, proteins, water, mineral salts and vitamins. Not only must there be a sufficient quantity of these foods, but they must also be present in their correct proportions.*

The same lesson recommends the following daily amounts of carbohydrates, fats, and protein for an average adult man:

carbohydrates	500g
fats	80g
protein	70g

Small amounts of minerals and vitamins, and, of course, plenty of water, are also required. We should not forget roughage, which is not itself digested, but which passes through the body, cleaning the system and aiding the digestive process.

Here are some sources of different food types. This is only a brief, simplified list. Many foods contain more than one of these items. If you want to know more about diet and nutrition, your local library should contain a wealth of material on the subject:

protein	meat, fish, mushrooms, cheese, milk, yogurt, nuts, pulses (beans, lentils, peas, etc.)
fats	butter, margarine, cooking oil, fatty meats, cheese, milk
carbohydrates	potatoes, bread, rice, maize, pasta, oatmeal, breakfast cereals, bananas
vitamins	fresh (raw) fruit and vegetables, fish, meat
roughage	fresh fruit and vegetables, brown bread, whole grains, bran
minerals	traces in various foods

Make sure you eat plenty of fresh food. Frozen foods, chips, takeaways and sweet, fizzy drinks are OK in small quantities, but none of them should play a major role in your diet.

If you don't eat fish, you should always buy iodated salt (salt with iodine added). Fish is the only natural source of iodine. And if you are a vegetarian you should ensure that you eat enough protein. And if for religious, moral, medical or other reasons you have further restrictions on what you eat, you should seek professional advice from a doctor or a dietician.

And finally, a few words about alcohol, caffeine, sleeping pills and drugs. If you are on medication, follow your doctor's instructions closely. Find out if the medicine you are taking has any side effects that could affect your studies, especially if you will be still taking it at exam time. If so, inform the exam centre in writing in advance, or if this is impossible, inform the invigilator on the day. If possible get a doctor's note explaining the situation.

Try to avoid taking sleeping tablets while you are studying. They reduce your awareness, even during the day. If you get anxious easily, try reducing the amount of coffee and tea that you drink: caffeine is a powerful stimulant. Try herbal teas, in particular camomile tea, instead. And it's best not to drink alcohol at all while you are studying. In quantity, alcohol leads to forgetfulness and can cause permanent brain damage. You may feel more confident, but you will study less efficiently.

ACTIVITY 6

1. Keep a list of everything you eat and drink for a week.
2. Include a note of approximate quantities.
3. Decide whether you think you are eating a healthy diet or not.
4. If not, make adjustments to your diet as necessary.
5. Take your list to your doctor or to a dietician for advice if you are unsure about any aspect of your diet.

Take plenty of exercise

Stress accumulates in our muscles unless we do something to prevent it. If we don't get regular exercise, our muscles become tighter and tighter. A gradual programme of exercise will help to make your muscles smoother and suppler.

Never launch into a vigorous exercise routine without preparation. It will do you more harm than good. Like studying, exercising must be a gradual and regular process. As suggested in Chapter 2, Section C, you should set aside periods for some form of exercise when designing your Study Plan.

Massage

Massage is a wonderful way of making your body supple and relaxed. If you know anyone who can give you a massage, ask them to do so. They may even be able to teach you how to return the favour!

Your back is really the only part of your body that you can't massage yourself, however. Try massaging the muscles of your face, for example. It's amazing how much more relaxed and refreshed you will feel after five minutes of gentle facial massage.

The muscles of your neck and upper back are also within your reach. Stress certainly seems to accumulate in this region of the body, especially if you spend long periods sitting at a desk, or driving, and even more so if you don't get much exercise.

You can also try massaging your arms, hands and fingers, and your legs, feet and toes. The important thing is, whether massaging your own or someone else's body, be gentle, and stop if it begins to hurt.

There's a wonderful book about massage. Most of the exercises are ones for which you don't need anybody else's help. It's called *Bodylife*, by Arthur Balaskas (London: Sidgwick & Jackson, 1977). See if you can find it in your local library.

Sleep

Only you know how much sleep you need. Most people need at least six hours, and few people really need more than 10, although people who are depressed can sometimes sleep all night and most of the next day.

You must find the right balance for yourself. Don't allow your studies, or any other activity, to deprive you of the sleep you need. This is especially important in the run-up to your exams.

If you get backache, you probably need some exercise. It may also be that your bed is no good. Old beds can become lumpy. If this has happened to your bed, you need to get a new one! A cheaper alternative is to buy a one-inch thick piece of chipboard the same area as your mattress, and place this between your mattress and the base of the bed.

C ADOPTING AN INTEGRATED APPROACH

Your studies need to fit into an overall routine, which includes all aspects of your life: your job (if you are working), your home life, your physical and mental health, your self-image, your attitude to your studies, your hobbies and leisure time, your family, colleagues and friends.

ACTIVITY 7

1. Keep a record of how you spend your time for a week, under the following headings:

   a sleeping
   b eating (including preparing food)
   c working (your job)
   d travelling to and from work, etc.
   e watching TV
   f exercising, including yoga, tai chi, sport, walking, etc.
   g other leisure activities, hobbies, etc.
   h studying

2. At the end of the week, compare your record with your Study Plan. How closely are you keeping to your Study Plan? Do you need to make any adjustments, either to your Study Plan or to the way you actually spend your time?

ACTIVITY 8

In this activity some Oxford Open Learning students are going to describe the problems they have finding time for their studies. Read what each one has to say and then write a few notes, giving your suggestions.

Phillipa says: 'I started a new part time job recently. That left me with less time than before to do my studying. So I've told all my friends to leave me alone until after the exams. I won't have time for anything except studying until then.'

Alan says: 'None of my mates are studying and they always want to drag me off to the pub when work is over. I try to say 'No', but it never seems to help. I don't know what to do about it.'

Ibrahim says: 'I do a lot of travelling around Britain by train and car for my job, and it doesn't leave me with much time for studying. What can I do about it?'

Shefali says: 'My problem is that no one seems to recognise the importance of my studies. Most of my friends aren't studying at present, and my family doesn't offer much support. I need a place where I can be alone. What can I do?'

D IF THINGS GO WRONG

If things are going wrong in your studies and you don't know what to do, don't panic! Take a short break and try to relax. Then re-read the following parts of Chapter 4, to see whether your problem is covered by any of them:

Section A	Thinking of suspending your studies?
Section A	Thinking of giving up altogether?
Section C	People who disrupt your studies
Section C	People who may be able to help you with your studies
Section D	Your money back if you fail

If none of this information helps, or even if some of it does, contact your tutor to discuss whatever is worrying you. Remember, while your tutor's main job is to provide advice about the subject you are studying, he/she is also available as a source of encouragement and moral support. You've already put a lot of effort into your studies — don't throw it all away because of a problem that actually can be solved!

One day at a time: remember that if things are going badly, you can't fix everything at once. You need to break the problem into smaller pieces and tackle these one at a time. You tutor may even be able to help you to do this, if you can't manage it alone. And if you feel miserable, try to focus on what needs to be done, instead of on your own emotions. Keeping yourself busy can often take your mind off other problems, and if you're *usefully* busy, you might even be starting to solve them!

ACTIVITY 9

1. Make a list of all the problems you face in your studies. Make your list as specific as possible. Vague, generalised statements, such as 'It's all too difficult' or 'I just don't have enough time' are not very helpful.

2. Try to think of practical ways in which you can overcome these difficulties.

3. Discuss your problems and possible solutions with your family, colleagues, or friends - anyone whom you feel you can trust.

4. If you want to, telephone your tutor to discuss any of these problems.

5. Talk to your tutor, especially if there are any problems you have identified, for which you cannot think of any solution.

6 PLANNING YOUR REVISION

A GETTING STARTED

Revising how to revise

We have mentioned revision many times already. If you have worked through most or all of the activities, you will have picked up many helpful hints that will enable you to prepare for the exams effectively. Whether or not you have done so, it will probably be worthwhile to look again at Sections B and C of Chapter 2 and most of Chapter 3 before reading through this chapter in detail.

In particular, Activities 5, 6 and 7 from Chapter 2, Section C will be of great help to you when planning your revision. Whether or not you have done these activities before, I suggest that you do them now.

ACTIVITY 1

1. Do (or redo) Activities 5, 6 and 7 of Chapter 2, Section C.

2. If you have done them before, and have kept a record of your previous responses, do not look at those responses until you have done the activities a second time.

3. Compare your previous responses with your current responses.

Now use the numbering and lettering system described in Activity 4 of Chapter 2, Section B to identify which are your strongest and weakest topics on the syllabus.

At this stage your interest level is much less important than how much you know, but you may not need to know every single topic on the syllabus in order to pass with a good grade.

It is difficult to generalise about this, so you should telephone your tutor to discuss the matter before making any decisions. If your tutor agrees that you can leave certain topics out of your revision plan, you can take your level of interest into account when deciding which ones to omit.

By the time you have completed Activity 1 above (Activities 5, 6 and 7 of Chapter 2, Section C) you should have a clear picture of what parts of the syllabus you are confident about, and which parts you are less familiar with. Think carefully about how best to divide your revision time among the various topics. Ensure that you devote enough time to the less familiar ones.

Now that you have completed the activities grouped together under Activity 1 above, you should *prioritise* your revision. You have already decided which topics need most of your attention. These are your highest priority.

Some students will choose to begin by revising their most difficult topics, and keep the easier ones for later. Other students will prefer to work through the topics in the same order in which they first studied them, taking care to spend more time on the difficult topics than on the easier ones. Still others may like to alternate easier and more difficult topics. If you opt for this approach, start with an easier topic!

ACTIVITY 2

1. Examine your recent responses to Activity 4 of Chapter 2, Section B.
2. Choose which revision order you want to follow:
    a. starting with the most difficult and ending with the easiest;
    b. in the order in which you studied them originally;
    c. starting with an easy topic and then alternating difficult and easy topics.
3. Write out a list of the topics and sub-topics in the order in which you plan to revise them.

Be sure that you also copy out the letter and number coding (indicating interest and difficulty) for easy reference.

Remember if the revision sequence you choose seems not to be working, you can return to this activity and try a different sequence, as long as you don't leave it too late!

Changing your Study Plan

The next phase involves changing your existing Study Plan. Ideally, you should have review sessions already incorporated into your Study Plan.

Starting about two months before the exams however, you will need to make significant changes to your Study Plan. You will be doing far less new work than before, and eventually none at all. Correspondingly, the amount of revision time needs to increase, until at the latest a month before the exams, all your study time will be spent on revision.

The best way to design a new Study Plan to cater for your revision needs is to go back to Chapter 2, Section B, and redo Activity 3, this time with revision firmly in mind.

ACTIVITY 3

1. Take the list of revision topics, arranged in your intended sequence, which you completed in Activity 2 of this chapter.

2. Redo Activity 3 of Chapter 2, Section B, with this list in mind.

3. Count the number of weeks you have left before the exam.

4. Fit your list of revision topics into your Study Plan.

5. Allocate more time for the topics you have identified as difficult topics, than for the easier ones.

6. You now have a detailed revision timetable.

Either:

7. Telephone your tutor and describe your revision timetable. Ask your tutor's advice about your allocation of time to each topic.

Or:

8. Post your tutor a copy of your revision timetable. Send it first class. Include a note asking for your tutor's comments. Give times when you will be available for your tutor to telephone you.

Revision skills

What skills do you need to be able to revise effectively? Revision skills are simply certain study skills put to a specific purpose. If you have worked through Chapter 3, you will have had plenty of practice in the relevant skills.

Of course, not every subject requires exactly the same skills, either for initial learning or for revision. Which study skills do you think are the most useful when it comes to revising your subject?

ACTIVITY 4

1. Look at the skills listed in Section A of Chapter 3.
2. If you need to refresh your memory about any of these skills, look up the relevant part of either Section B (*Receptive Skills*) or Section C (*Productive Skills*) of Chapter 3.
3. List the skills you think will be the most useful to you in your revision.
4. If necessary, redo some or all of the activities in Chapter 3 that relate to the skills you have chosen.
5. Can you think of any other skills that do not appear on the list in Chapter 3, Section A, which will be important in your revision?
6. If you want to, telephone your tutor to discuss your list of revision skills.

You could argue that all the skills listed in Chapter 3 are relevant to revision. However, at the end of this chapter I have given a list of skills that are generally important in revision. Compare your ideas with my list, remembering that different subjects may require different skills, and that my list is intended to be only a very general guide.

B GETTING CREATIVELY INVOLVED

What good revision isn't

Many students think that revision involves simply reading through everything they have studied. Often there is not a pen or notebook in sight: just books and study packs.

The problem is that very few people have a photographic memory. If *you* do, you're lucky. For the rest of us, sitting with books and desperately attempting to absorb the contents is unlikely to achieve much. This is because, for most of us, such behaviour is too *passive*.

What good revision is

Most of us learn best by *doing*. We need to be engaged, or actively involved, in something for it to make sense. This is why both your study pack and this book include so many *activities*.

Imagine trying to teach someone to use a computer or drive a car just by giving them instructions. It would be hopeless! These tasks need the practical and active involvement of the student before real learning can take place.

Some subjects require more active participation than others. But the principle that doing is better than not doing holds good for all subjects, and especially during your revision period.

This section examines ways of making your revision a more *active* process. Inevitably, this section will repeat some of the ideas that have been covered in earlier chapters, but it will place them in the context of your revision programme.

A time and place for revision

In Section C of Chapter 1, we looked at the equipment and the setting you need to study efficiently. There are no basic differences when it comes to revision. However, now might be a good time to tidy up your study area, particularly if you have accumulated a lot of clutter. But don't throw away your notes by mistake!

As your revision timetable may be different to your original Study Plan, you should also tell your friends and family about the changes to your schedule. It is important that your revision sessions proceed without interruptions.

Taking up an active role

Spend half an hour now and then on the notes you made on a difficult topic some time ago, so that no single topic ever gets completely forgotten. If you haven't been doing this, start now!

ACTIVITY 5

1. Choose a topic from early on in your course that you want to revise.
2. If you have kept a study journal, look up your notes on this topic. Check how much time you spent studying it. Also note any difficulties you faced at that time.
3. Gather up your notes on the topic and turn to the relevant section of your study pack.

4. If you have highlighted the main points in the study pack, compare the highlighted points to your notes.

5. If you haven't already done so, highlight the main points now.

6. Next, re-read any SATs or TMAs that you have written that relate to this topic.

7. For SATs, check the Suggested Answers against your own.

8. For TMAs, read your tutor's comments. Compare your answers to the Suggested Answers sent to you by Oxford Open Learning.

9. Next, condense your notes on this topic. You may wish to do this over several stages.

10. Ultimately, you want to get the main points for each topic onto a few sheets of paper. Many students like to use cards, which should be A5 or smaller in size.

11. You can invent new symbols or abbreviations at this stage of your revision. You can design charts or diagrams. You may also want to use colour coding to sort your notes into different categories. Use whichever method works best for you.

Condense, condense, condense

I once started with 10 A4 pages of history notes. I couldn't remember the contents, so I highlighted the main points. Then I made a new set of notes, ignoring everything that was not highlighted, and reduced the 10 pages to only two.

Next, I highlighted the 'main points of the main points' and copied these onto three pieces of card, which I called *prompt cards.* Of course I kept the longer, more detailed notes in case I needed to refer to them to clarify anything I couldn't remember from the prompt cards.

The advantages of using cards are that they are small, transportable and more durable than paper. When you have condensed your notes, look at them regularly. Carry some of them around with you, in case you have a few minutes spare while waiting for a bus, or standing in a Post Office queue.

Once you have reduced your revision notes to the barest essentials, attempt a question or two on this topic from a past exam paper. Section C of this chapter (below) deals with how to use past exam papers for revision purposes.

There are other ways to liven up your revision. If you have a cassette player fitted with a microphone, you can make a tape of your notes. You can then play back the tape when you are doing other activities, such as exercising, eating your supper, or travelling to work.

You can even play a tape to yourself when you go to bed at night. If you set the volume low, it should not prevent you from sleeping, and there is a good chance that your mind will be receptive to this information while you are asleep.

Divide your revision into manageable units. Some of the activities earlier in this chapter show you how to do this. Inevitably, revision is more pressured than ordinary studying. You know that the exams are coming up soon, and there is a lot to do. All the more reason to have a clearly defined target for each revision session!

If possible, build a set of self-test questions into the end of each revision session to check that it has been successful. Keep a checklist of revision topics (see Activity 2 above) and tick off each one as you complete it. This gives you a visual record of revision progress. It will also improve your self-confidence. Often enough, confidence is just the result of being clear-headed and organised about your revision!

Other aids to revision

You've probably noticed that there is a massive revision 'industry' that is re-launched every April, in time for the June exams. At this time the newspapers are full of advertisements for revision aids. There may also be late night TV programmes aimed at revision.

Identify your specific needs, and shop around with care if you really feel you need this extra help. But remember that you already have this *How to Study* guide, and a good study pack, such as those provided by Oxford Open Learning, will have organised all the information you need, and you may become confused if you switch to a completely different approach at this late stage.

ACTIVITY 6

1. In this activity, you will use what you have learned in Sections A and B of this chapter to give advice to some Oxford Open Learning students.
2. Each student has a problem with their revision.
3. Read about their problems and write brief notes suggesting what the student should do to improve their chances in the exam.

Phillipa says: 'Now the exams are approaching, I spend six hours every day reading through my Study Pack and my textbooks. I want to remember as much information as possible, but I just don't seem to be able to. What should I do?'

Ibrahim says: 'I've worked hard at my course and I've made loads of notes. In fact, I've got so many notes that I can't find anything when I need it. All my papers are piled on top of my wardrobe. I pull out some of my notes from time to time, but nothing seems to connect up with anything else. What do you think I should do?'

Alan says: 'This revision lark is easy. I've finished the course and done all my TMAs. I'm going to take a couple of weeks' holiday now. I won't need more than a week or so to do my revision, will I?'

Sarah says: 'Revision is just a question of memory. I'm going to spend all my time re-reading my notes and copying them out. Then I'll be sure to have all the information I need in my mind on the day of the exam. Doing practice questions is a waste of time. Do you agree?'

Shefali says: 'I'm taking my revision very seriously. I don't have time to go out and have fun at the moment. I'm going to do 12 hours revision every day. The night before the exam I'm going to make a huge pot of coffee and stay up all night to make sure that all the facts I need are in my head. That should do the trick! What do you think?'

C EXAM PRACTICE AND CHECKING FOR RELEVANCE

Practice makes perfect

This section emphasises the need to round off your revision of each topic with plenty of exam practice. Look again at Activity 5 in Section B above. Only by getting plenty of practice under exam conditions will you be sure to cope efficiently with the exams themselves.

Exam conditions differ in many ways from normal study conditions. Some of these are dealt with in Chapter 7 below, which is concerned with exam enrolment and preparation.

There are two main ways in which exam conditions differ: you are generally not allowed to have any reference materials, books or notes with you; and, you have to work against a strict time limit.

In Chapter 4, Section A, we advised you to attempt your TMAs without reference to your notes, partly to help your tutor to identify any weaknesses in your understanding, and partly to give you practice in one aspect of exam conditions. No mention was made of a time limit there, however. The twin restrictions of no notes, and a strict time limit, are two of the factors that make exams particularly challenging.

Activity 7 (below) helps you take the revision process further. In this activity you will answer a question from a past paper under exam conditions. Before you start Activity 7, however, a word of warning.

One of the most serious failings of students in the exam is writing *irrelevant* information. All too often, instead of paying attention to the wording of the question, students simply scribble down everything they can remember about the topic, whether it is relevant or not. *Always*, therefore, spend a few moments thinking about the terms of reference of the question before you start planning your answer.

ACTIVITY 7

First, do Activity 5 in Section B of this chapter for a selected revision topic. Be sure to read all the instructions below before you begin.

1. Read through two or three past exam papers. If possible, set aside one or two others for use as mock exam papers later (see Chapter 7, Section B). Do not look at the paper(s) you set aside.

2. If you still don't have any past exam papers, make arrangements to acquire some immediately, before it's too late! (See Chapter 2, Section C for details.)

3. Mark any questions that cover the topic that you have been revising.

4. Note the time limit that applies to each question.

5. Copy each relevant question onto a separate piece of card or small square of paper.

6. Write the time limit in brackets at the end of each question.

7. Shuffle the questions and pick one out at random.

8. Highlight the key words in the question.

9. Fix these words in your mind to make sure that every aspect of your planned answer is *relevant* to the question.

10. Spend between 5 and 15 minutes brainstorming, mind-mapping and planning your answer. (How long you spend depends on the time allocation for the whole question.)

11. If you can't remember how to do brainstorming and mind-mapping, re-read the relevant part of Section C of Chapter 3 above first.

12. When planning your answer, keep checking for relevance.

13. Write an answer to this question, without reference to any notes or other study materials, keeping within the time limit.

14. When you have finished, look over your notes again, and if necessary, your study pack.

15. Try to judge whether you have answered the question adequately or not.

16. If not, look for information or ideas that you feel you should have included.

Note: item no. 10 above is not necessary in the case of certain Mathematics and other science questions.

ACTIVITY 8

You should always attempt several past questions on each main topic before you sit the exam, especially if you have attempted one question and feel you haven't done very well.

1. If you are not satisfied with the answer you have just completed, spend another hour or so revising your notes.

2. Set aside the question you have already answered.

3. Then shuffle your pack of remaining exam questions on the same topic.

4. Follow the same procedure as for Activity 6 above.

Mobile revision cards

Finally, here is another reason for copying out questions from past exam papers onto small pieces of paper or card. You can carry a few of these in your pockets and refer to them when your mind is not otherwise occupied. This might be while walking to the shops, travelling by bus or train, or waiting for your boyfriend or girlfriend (who is always late).

"CREDIT CARDS... NO! REVISION CARDS... YES!"

At these times, you can *think* about how you would tackle a particular question. It doesn't matter that you don't write anything down (although if you have a notebook and pencil with you, you can).

If you've spent some time thinking about a question, you'll be amazed how much easier it becomes to write an answer to it later. It will seem more familiar from the beginning, and therefore much easier to brainstorm and plan. As I said earlier: time is precious, so make the most of it, especially when you are in the midst of your revision.

D GETTING HELP

This brief section should be read in conjunction with the last part of Chapter 4, Section C, entitled *People who may be able to help with your studies*.

We have looked at ways of making your revision *active* rather than *passive*. If you can find a helper, you may be able to make your revision programme more *interactive*. At the very least, you can telephone your tutor to discuss any problems you encounter in your revision programme.

If you *are* able to get together with other students, or with helpers, there are various ways in which you can enhance your revision. A study group with other students would enable you to share ideas, not only about understanding your coursework, but also about how to revise effectively.

One member of the group may discover a useful way of describing a particular process, for example. Another may invent a system of symbols or a mnemonic which helps to remember a formula. Another may find a way of representing 500 words of difficult text as an easy-to-read flow chart or tree diagram.

By pooling your resources you improve everyone's chances of success. Remember: you can afford to cooperate, because you are not competing with one another. It is quite possible for all members of the study group to pass.

If you have managed to reduce your revision notes to a series of cards, you can invent a quiz to test yourself on specific questions. You don't need to be a member of a study group to do this: you can formulate the questions and answers yourself. (Double-check that the answers are correct!) And all you need is one person who is willing to ask you the questions and check the answers.

Suggested list of revision skills (see ACTIVITY 4 above)

Receptive skills

- Skimming
- Scanning
- Using abbreviations
- Making notes
- Summarising

Productive skills

- Brainstorming, mind-maps and planning an essay
- Breaking up large tasks into smaller ones
- Recycling your studies
- Improving your memory
- Assessing your own progress

7 PREPARING FOR THE EXAMS

A ENROLLING FOR THE EXAMS

Examination arrangements (locally enrolled students)

If you are enrolled at your local college of further education, your college will normally advise you of the arrangements made for you to sit the examinations. Please ignore the remainder of Section A of this chapter and continue reading from Section B.

Examination arrangements (students who are not enrolled at a CFE)

Unless you are already enrolled at a local college of further education (CFE), you will need to make your own arrangements to sit the examination. Neither Oxford Open Learning nor your tutor can make the necessary arrangements for you.

You should make enquiries locally, for instance at the nearest CFE to where you live. Most CFEs will be only too pleased to help. Your exam board may also be able to give you advice on a suitable local exam centre. The contact addresses and telephone numbers for the various exam boards are given in Chapter 2, Section C.

Organise your enrolment at the earliest opportunity, and at least six months before the date of your examination. This means enrolling by January at the latest (and preferably the previous November) for the June exams.

If you plan to take the exams in January, you should enrol by September of the previous year. Another good reason for making examination arrangements as early as possible is that it will help you to focus on a deadline and motivate you to finish your studies on time.

With some syllabuses, you will need to plan even further ahead because of coursework requirements, etc. The introduction to your course at the beginning of your study pack should make it clear whether or not this will be necessary.

It is likely that you will be charged a fee by the school or college where the exams are being held. This covers the cost of administration, etc.

Some schools and colleges may not hold exams for the particular examination board that you are working towards. If so, you have two alternatives:

1. ask at other schools or colleges until you find one which *does* hold the right examination;
2. check with your tutor and with the introduction to the course to see whether you can take the examination as set by a different board. In most GCSE subjects, there is a great deal of similarity between the exams set by different boards.

You may need to be patient and contact a number of colleges in order to find one that offers the syllabus that you have followed. There are many schools and colleges to choose from, however, so you can be confident of finding one, as long as you are willing to look around. If you live in a remote place you should be prepared to travel to the nearest city to sit your exams.

Here are some experiences of Oxford Open Learning students who wanted to enter for their exams.

Phillipa says: 'As I live in a big city there are a lot of schools and colleges around. I didn't want to sit my exams with a lot of schoolkids, so straight after the New Year I tried one of the CFEs nearby. The first one wasn't very helpful, but the second one had plenty of space and was very happy to fit me in for the exams in June.'

Ibrahim says: 'I enrolled at my local college of further education (where my tutor works full-time), so the college took care of all of my exam arrangements for me. I didn't need to do anything.'

Alan says: 'I wish I'd read all the advice and information provided by Oxford Open Learning earlier. I thought all I had to do was get on with the course. I didn't bother much about anything else. I didn't realise I had to make my own exam arrangements until March, and by then it was too late. So now I've missed the chance to do the exams until next year. It's my own fault for not reading the information properly.'

Sarah says: 'I realised that it is sometimes tricky to find an exam venue, so I started looking around in November for a place to write my exams the following June. At first my local college claimed that it was impossible for me to enter, because

of the GCSE Business Studies coursework requirement, but I eventually persuaded them that this was not a problem.'

Shefali says: 'I like to be organised and I usually am, but I just plain forgot about entering for the exams. Thank goodness my friend, who is also studying with Oxford Open Learning, reminded me. It was nearly the end of January, but I was able to find a school close to where I live that would let me enter, so I've sorted out the problem now.'

Entering as an external candidate

Many home learners belong to a special category for exam purposes – the external candidate. What is an external candidate? This is a candidate who is taking their final exams at a college (or school) where they are *not* enrolled.

If you *are* enrolled at the college where you are taking the written papers, you are classed as an internal candidate. If coursework is required, this will mean that a tutor at that college *must* mark the coursework.

External candidates normally have their coursework marked 'direct' by the exam board – an option which is not open to internal candidates.

Not all college examination officers are fully aware of all these details. Some may say, 'Sorry, we can't let you sit the exam here. Coursework is compulsory for your subject and because we didn't teach you, we can't mark or authenticate your coursework.'

This is incorrect. The college taking your exam entry does not need to mark or authenticate your coursework. The exam board marks it and your regular tutor (who may work for a different college) authenticates it (i.e. confirms that it is your own work).

So don't take this kind of 'no' for an answer. Convince the exams officer that you *are allowed* to enter as an external candidate and that coursework is not a problem. Ask the college to check with the exam board if they don't believe you.

The exams officer at the exam centre where you want to sit your exams may turn you down on the grounds that the exam centre doesn't hold exams in the syllabus that you want to write. They won't be willing to set up an exam just for you. This is just bad luck, and it means that you will have to try somewhere else.

If you do enter as an external candidate, you will find yourself communicating directly with the exam board. Do not worry about this. The exam board will tell you exactly what they want, and when. Do not miss the deadlines. The exam board will not hold back deadlines just for you.

If your syllabus does not require coursework, you may find that exams officers are a lot happier to let you enter – always assuming that they are holding exams in your particular syllabus.

Changing your examination date

Circumstances change and you may decide at some point that your target examination date is no longer realistic. Your tutor may also have reason to advise you that you are not ready to take the exam at the anticipated time.

Usually this is not a problem. In most cases, there is plenty of time to take the examination and our tutors will continue to support you throughout your studies. Generally, it is possible for you to take the exam up to three years after your original enrolment with Oxford Open Learning. A student who enrols in 2000, for instance, may take the examination at any sitting up to and including June 2003. This arrangement is designed to offer you the maximum flexibility, and to give you plenty of time should you need it.

You have to bear in mind, however, that it is not *always* possible to change your exam date to suit your needs. Syllabuses sometimes change so much that the existing course no longer offers appropriate preparation. Occasionally syllabuses are heavily revised or replaced altogether.

So, you might be unlucky. For example, you might originally have aimed for the 2000 examination. Later on, however, you decide that you want to delay sitting the exam until 2001, only to be told that it is not possible to do so because the syllabus you have been studying is no longer available.

Unfortunately, no organisation can guarantee that such situations will not occur. This is because syllabuses are only made available about two years before the exams to which they relate. So, to be on the safe side, it is best if you aim for an exam date no more than two years from the date of your enrolment.

Oxford Open Learning is one organisation that does its best to cater for such changes. If a syllabus still exists at the time you want to sit your exam, but has changed significantly, you will be able to buy Oxford Open Learning's revised course (if one is offered) at half the normal price. This will enable you to continue studying without incurring undue expense.

Your tutor will advise you if you are likely to face this kind of problem. So if you think you may have to postpone taking the exam, let your tutor know as early as you can and discuss the possible implications.

Under some circumstances, it may be necessary to complete additional enrolment forms to take you through the extra academic year. Your college (or Oxford Open Learning) will let you know if this is necessary.

B GETTING USED TO EXAM CONDITIONS

Be prepared!

Getting ready to take exams requires a gradual and systematic programme of preparation. If you were going to take part in an Olympic athletics event, you wouldn't wait until the week before to start training.

The same goes for exams: you need a gradual, disciplined build-up to the event. At least a month, and preferably two months, before your exams take place, you need to go into training.

If you've worked through this book, done most of the activities and followed most of the advice, you will already be well prepared. If you've just skimmed through, however, or not read much of this *How to Study* guide, I suggest that you look at Chapter 6 in some detail before you proceed with this chapter. In particular, you should read Sections B and C and work through Activities 5, 7 and 8. These provide the necessary practice to prepare you for the activities in this section.

Simulate exam conditions

Activities 5, 7 and 8 in Chapter 6 are designed to get you used to writing individual questions under exam conditions. You should try to get plenty of practice at this. However, you also need a certain amount of practice at writing a whole exam.

A runner who only ever practised running 100 metres would certainly not be prepared to run a 400 metres race. Although most of your practice sessions will deal with one question, you should also attempt at least one whole mock exam. For this, the questions you face should be ones you have never seen before, as they will be in the exam itself.

ACTIVITY 1

Don't leave this activity until a few days before the actual exam. Try to schedule it a couple of weeks before you write, if possible.

1. If you have set aside a past exam paper to use as a mock exam, you should find it now. Do not look at any of the questions yet.
2. If you don't have a past exam paper that you have not yet looked at, you should spend some time taking different questions on different topics from different past exam papers. In other words, you should compile your own mock exam paper with questions taken from whatever past papers you have available. If possible, choose questions that you have not thought much about before. Certainly do not include any questions which you have already answered. Make sure that all the details of your own mock exam paper (number and choice of questions, time limit etc.) are exactly as they will be in the real exam.
3. For this activity, it is *essential* that you simulate exam conditions as closely as possible. You should attempt the same number of questions, in the same time limit, as in the actual exam. In particular, make sure that you are not disturbed while you are writing your mock exam.

ACTIVITY 2

This activity follows on from Activity 1 and should be done the next day, or within a few days.

1. When you have finished writing your mock exam, set it aside until the next day. Do not look at it or even think about it until then.

2. The following day, re-read the question paper. This time there is no time limit. Try to imagine that you are the examiner, and that the answer paper was written by someone else.

3. Read your answers carefully.

4. Note any language errors or mistakes of fact.

5. Tick any good points.

6. Don't attempt to give your work a mark, but try to see it from the examiner's point of view.

7. Finally, make notes on anything you would change.

"IT'S NO GOOD – I CAN'T READ YOUR WRITING!"

Writing a mock exam can be nearly as stressful as the exam itself. It's certainly quite tiring. So I wouldn't recommend that you do this too often. However, simulating exam conditions is the best way of preparing yourself for the actual experience. If you can find the time and the energy to go through this routine *twice* before you sit the real exam, you will be properly *hardened* to exam conditions. The likelihood of your panicking or being unable to cope will then be reduced. So if you have the opportunity and the willpower, repeat Activities 1 and 2 with a different past or mock exam paper.

C HOW TO SPEND THE LAST FEW DAYS BEFORE THE EXAM

The build-up to the exam

In the last few days before you sit the exam, you may need to adjust your revision timetable to focus on your weakest topics. (Don't neglect your stronger topics altogether, however.)

At this stage you should condense your revision notes further and further, so that your revision cards or sheets of paper act as prompts to remind you of the more detailed information that you have recorded in your fuller notes.

The time is now past (unless you are feeling very energetic) to attempt a whole mock exam. You might want additional practice in answering individual questions under exam conditions, however, or at least brainstorming and planning such answers.

The remainder of your revision time should be devoted to recalling information and ideas, and reducing your prompts to the barest minimum. If anyone is available to test you on the contents of your revision notes, now is the time to ask them for help (see Chapter 6, Section D).

Now, more than ever, you need to make sure you get enough food, exercise and sleep (see Chapter 5, Section B). If you are getting anxious, try some of the suggestions in Chapter 5, Section A.

Mental preparation is very important. Remember that exams are not usually as difficult as most students believe, especially if you have revised your course thoroughly.

Nobody is trying to trick you into failing. The examiners do their best to be fair. They are always thoroughly trained by the exam boards. They are also supplied with detailed marking guidelines to ensure that as far as possible, all candidates are treated alike.

Some students talk about *losing* marks for making mistakes. Actually this is impossible! Think about it. All candidates start off with blank answer papers and zero marks. Don't forget that as you write you exam, you are *gaining* marks, not losing them.

Getting to the exam venue

This may sound silly, but I think it's important to mention it. Some students get so wrapped up in their revision programme that they forget to think about the practicalities of transporting themselves to the exam venue on the day of the exam. If the exam is being held in a place that is very familiar to you, this is probably not a problem.

But if you don't know the area, or the exact location, of the exam venue, you would be well advised to investigate these details thoroughly, and well in advance of the date of the exam. It might even be worth doing a practice run, travelling the entire journey (at the same time of day as you will travel on the exam day itself), to see how long it takes. In many congested cities in the UK, rush-hour traffic moves very slowly indeed!

When you arrive at the venue, check exactly where in the building your exam will take place. It is quite possible that there will be several exams taking place at the same time on the same day, but in different rooms. Or if very many candidates are sitting the same exam, candidates may be allocated to a room according to their surname or their candidate number.

eXam
centre

Towards the examination day

- Check that you know the correct time of the examination.
- Make sure that you know the location of your examination centre, and the room in which the examination is to be held.
- Check that you have your candidate's examination number.
- Ensure that you have proof of your identity (a passport or other document that includes a photograph).
- Take a watch or clock with you.
- Ensure that you have all the pencils, pens and other equipment that you are likely to need.
- If you use a calculator, ensure that it conforms to the specifications permitted in the exam.

Last minute preparations

On the morning before the day of your exam, spend a couple of hours, in half-hour sessions, looking through your notes or cards.

Pack you bag, with all the equipment you need for the exam (see list above). Make sure you have a reliable watch with you. Exam venues will normally display a clock, but this may not be easily visible from every seat in the room.

If possible, take the rest of the day off. Make sure you get enough nutritious food and enough sleep that night. Otherwise, try to forget about your studies. Watch a programme on TV, or pursue your favourite hobby. Before you go to bed, get out the clothes you will wear (this just saves time and prevents additional panic the next morning).

Don't spend time with people who are likely to upset you or make you feel more stressed. *Don't* spend this day trying to reorganise your love life. And *don't* spend the evening before your exam in the pub!

D WHAT TO DO ON THE DAY OF THE EXAM

- Arrive in plenty of time - don't rush yourself.
- If you feel nervous, do the breathing exercise described in Activity 1 of Chapter 6.
- Carefully check all instructions regarding entering your name, candidate number, etc.
- Read the whole exam paper before you begin writing any answers. (Your unconscious mind will

be working out answers to other questions while your conscious mind tackles the first one.)

- Read all questions carefully to judge those you can answer best.
- Unless instructed otherwise, answer your best questions first. Nevertheless, make sure you also allow enough time to answer the questions that are less appealing.
- Attempt to answer all questions, except where the paper allows for choice - missing out compulsory questions will lead you to miss opportunities to score marks.
- Note (if necessary, underline) key words in the question you are answering. Make sure your answer addresses the question accurately. *Don't* simply repeat everything you know about the topic. Irrelevant answers are one of the main reasons why students score low marks in exams.
- Check the approximate time available for answering each question so that you don't run out of time.
- Number your answers clearly, exactly as they are numbered in the questions.
- Ensure that your handwriting is legible. Examiners get very impatient if they cannot read what you have written. An otherwise brilliant essay written in terrible handwriting may score very low marks. Even if your work can be read with effort, the examiner may mark you down, since such extra effort shouldn't be necessary.
- Make any alterations clearly.

- If possible, allow enough time to spend ten or fifteen minutes reading through and checking your answers before the end of the exam.
- If you are running out of time, remember that two half-answered questions are likely to score more marks than one complete answer and one question not answered at all. If time is a serious problem, skeleton notes or an outline of an answer are better than nothing at all.

Above all, don't worry! Relax! Provided you have worked well, your study pack will have fully prepared you. You can feel confident. Many Oxford Open Learning students have gained distinctions and 'A' grades, and many, many more have passed with flying colours.

If you have followed your study pack carefully, and have written all your Tutor-Marked Assignments, you should know your syllabus quite well. And if you have worked through some or most of *How to Study at Home the Oxford Open Learning Way*, you can be confident that you also have the study, revision and examination skills necessary to achieve your goal. So best wishes from everyone at Oxford Open Learning, and good luck in your exams!